UNDERST
REVELATION

PASTOR ANNALISE VAN RENSBURG

Photography by Petrus van Rensburg
Cover design by Shane Govender

Spirit Word Ministries

P.O. Box 10344

Klerksdorp

2570, South Africa

www.spiritword.org.za

ISBN 978-1-928434-06-1

Prophet Kobus
& Pastor Annalise
van Rensburg

$\mathcal{D}$EDICATION

I cannot but dedicate this book to my husband, Kobus van Rensburg, who did not only preach the living Word to us but showed us the way, by living the Word.

His love and dedication to his Saviour made the Word come alive for so many people. He loved sharing revelations from the Word, and his desire was for all to receive the life-giving, "Spirit Word".

We are so busy existing, that we are blinded to life itself. It was only after he passed on, that I realized how blessed we were to have walked with this awesome man of God.

I am forever grateful.

He made it look so easy, but his sincere love for God and a true hunger for the Word has touched so many. By the Spirit, he made the Word come alive, revealing the treasures hidden in the Word.

A tangible excitement and expectancy accompanied his preaching, and he always wanted to know: "Are you hearing?" Hearing is when the revelation drops. The services were permeated with such a high level of revelation from the Word, and miracles were inevitable. When it came to ministry, he went full throttle, never considering his own situation or condition.

He loved people, yet he never compromised the Word, that brought radical change in people's understanding of it. People were changed just by meeting him, for he had no condemnation towards anyone. Where ever I go people stop me and tell me stories of how their lives were touched and changed by him. We cannot help but miss Him, he carried the glory of God wherever He went.

I nearly fell off my chair, when one day, he turned to me and with a soft smile on his face said, "One day you will preach the book of Revelation, and it will bring radical change to people's understanding of the Word."Finally, this day has arrived. I can see that smile again. I miss him so much.

My prayer is that this book will create a hunger in you, a hunger to read and understand the finished work of Christ. May the blessing promised in this awesome book of Revelation, be your portion.

$\mathscr{F}$OREWORD

Pastor John Wasserman

Pastor of Airport Christian Fellowship, Johannesburg, South Africa

This book is unique...

'Unique' is a word often, lightly or flippantly used. It is ascribed to people or objects, amongst other things. But 'unique' can also be a word most aptly or pertinently spoken when referring to these same subjects.

The reason this book is unique, is not only found in it's subject matter, which incidentally is refreshingly different from all other books on Revelation but by the fact of it being written by Annalise van Rensburg.

Annalise is someone uniquely equipped by God to write this book. Years of investing herself in the Word of God and in the ministry of the late Prophet Kobus van Rensburg, has resulted in an understanding of this final letter in the Bible. She has gained a biblical perspective and insight into the mysteries of John's revelation. No-one can undertake the task of expounding Revelation unless they have an overview and grasp of the entire canon of scripture, from Genesis to Jude. Some of the early great Bible expositors correctly stated, that the Bible has enough light for its own interpretation. We don't need to go to extra-biblical sources or into historical records necessarily to gain an understanding of this, most misunderstood of all the books in the Bible. I am persuaded that Annalise has gained light on this subject.

You will do well to prayerfully and carefully read this study. Read it without prejudice or bias and allow the Spirit to challenge your theology and hence, to change your life.

Pastor Dave and Elbie Basson

Pastors of Kingdom Light Church, Capetown, South Africa

In Revelation 1:3 it says, there is a blessing to be had for those who read and understand this prophecy. Annalise Van Rensburg has not only made it her mission to understand Revelation but also it is her heart to make it known to others bringing them freedom and delivering them from fear . So right here and now she shares her many years of study and hard work. This is not another end time, fear creating edition of man's explanation of how Revelation fits into Armageddon and the beast and the number 666. No... No! Not at all!

This is an accurate "scripture declares scripture" portrayal of the finished work of the cross as it is the revelation of Jesus Christ.

A tracing of the mysterious, yet wonderful golden thread that runs through the scriptures from Genesis to Revelation proving and explaining symbols like trumpets, vials and horses. Giving definitions to numbers like 3, 4, 7, 1000 and 144000. All the while, keeping you captivated and ready for the next mystery to be revealed.

This is a must read! It will set you free from man's opinion and interpretation of the current news, political stand offs as relating to end times. A must for every bible student.

Thank you Annalise for persevering to give us this great book!

REFACE

Rev 1:3
Blessed is he that reads,
and they that hear the words of this prophecy,
and keep those things which are written therein:
for the time is at hand.

Most books written about the book of Revelation are so difficult to read, it seems to be ten times thicker than the book of Revelation itself. Most of these books leave us lost in the corridors of time. Generally, we are left feeling confused and inadequate to comprehend what John actually saw on the island of Patmos.

I intend for this to be an easy-to-read framework about the book of Revelation, in order to help you understand the Spirit of the Word and the visions that John saw. Revelation is not a separate book for some time in the future. You cannot understand Revelation without an understanding of the Word from the beginning.

This book is the only book with a promise of a blessing when you read it. That alone should indicate the importance of the book. It does not only promise a blessing, but the book also has a warning that nothing should be added or taken from its text.

> **Rev 22:18** For I testify unto every man that heareth the words of the prophecy of this book, If any man shall add unto these things, God shall add unto him the plagues that are written in this book:

> **Rev 22:19** And if any man shall take away from the words of the book of

this prophecy, God shall take away his part out of the book of life, and out of the holy city, and from the things which are written in this book.

Ever since the book was written, people tried to decipher the book and most people find themselves in a maze of natural interpretations, for a spiritual book. The Word will explain the Word, through the Holy Spirit that now dwells in believers. This is why we need the infilling and leading of the Spirit, for it is the only way that we will be free from adding and subtracting from this vision that was given to John.

> **Rev 1:1** The Revelation of Jesus Christ, which God gave unto him, to shew unto his servants, things which must shortly come to pass; and he sent and signified [it] by his angel unto his servant John.

• TO REVEAL, TO UNVEIL OR TO OPEN UP

The word used for Revelation is apocalypse and it means to opening up or to reveal. Revelation is the final revealing of the eternal purposes of Christ and His victory over evil, as well as the finishing of the work He started on the cross.

> **1 John 3:8** For this purpose the Son of God was manifested, that he might destroy the works of the devil.

God's intention for us is to understand His plans and purpose.

- Gabriel was sent to Daniel to bring understanding and knowledge concerning the visions he saw.

Dan 8:16 And I heard a man's voice between [the banks of] Ulai, which called, and said, Gabriel, make this [man] to understand the vision.

-In the book of Revelation, God himself revealed himself through His angel to his servant to John.

Rev 1:1 The Revelation of Jesus Christ, which God gave unto him, to shew unto his servants, things which must shortly come to pass; and he sent and signified [it] by his angel unto his servant John:

God wants His body, the church, to know His purposes and plans in order to grow into perfection, the full image and stature of the fullness of the Christ; not to hide in fear and prepare for doomsday.

Ironically, the book of Revelation is used incorrectly by evoking fear to try and scare people into salvation. In doing so, Satan is given authority that does not belong to him and the church is left powerless and deceived. Satan does not have the last say on the earth. That is totally twisting and perverting the message as well as the purposes of God revealed in the book of Revelation, as well as the whole Bible.

2 Tim 1:7 For God hath not given us the spirit of fear; but of power, and of love, and of a sound mind.

• GOD'S REDEMPTION PLAN

The entire Bible is all about one subject: Christ coming to do the will of the Father, through a Body that was prepared to bring the right seed into the earth in order for man to taste the goodness of God and to receive life; The Bible is the redemption story of mankind revealed.

Heb 10:7 Then said I, Lo, I come (in the volume of the book it is written of me,) to do thy will, O God.

However, the Son was only revealed in a specific time frame called the fullness of time.

Gal 4:4 But when the fullness of the time was come, God sent forth his Son, made of a woman, made under the law,

1 Tim 3:16 And without controversy great is the mystery of godliness: God was manifest in the flesh, justified in the Spirit, seen of angels, preached unto the Gentiles, believed on in the world, received up into glory.

The book of Revelation is very clear as to what it is about. It is not Revelations…, plural, but Revelation, singular. It is the revelation of one subject only; JESUS CHRIST the LORD. It contains the fulfillment and completion of the purposes of Christ, and how He accomplished that.

Rev 10:7 But in the days of the voice of the seventh angel, when he shall begin to sound, the mystery of God should be finished, as he hath declared to his servants the prophets.

• AS TIME GOES REVELATION GROWS

Please remember that revelation of the Word is progressive and time bound. There is a saying which is really true when it comes to revelation in the Word;

"WHEN THE STUDENT IS READY THE TEACHER APPEARS."

> 2 Pet 1:19 We have also a more, sure word of prophecy; whereunto ye do well that ye take heed, as unto a light that shineth in a dark place, until the day dawn, and the day star arise in your hearts:

Even the prophets did not precisely know or understand their own prophecies. They searched for what time the Spirit of Christ, which was in them, did signify.

> 1 Pet 1:10 Of which salvation the prophets have enquired and searched diligently, who prophesied of the grace [that should come] unto you:

> 1 Pet 1:11 Searching what, or what manner of time the Spirit of Christ which was in them did signify, when it testified beforehand the sufferings of Christ, and the glory that should follow.

God worked out His redemption plan throughout human history, yet the mysteries of God can only be understood when the Holy Spirit opens it up at His appointed time, to people that would "HEAR WHAT THE SPIRIT SAYS."

• HEAR WHAT THE SPIRIT SAYS

God is Spirit, and His eternal plans and purposes cannot be subject to our short-lived, imperfect, fleshly minds. The only way to understand the Word is by the Spirit. The Spirit gives us understanding in our own way and through our own filters.

God commanded John, the only apostle still alive, to write to the seven letters to the churches in Asia and the most important message to every church; is to hear with a spiritual ear:

"IF YOU HAVE AN EAR, HEAR WHAT THE SPIRIT SAYS."

We live in a time that those letters from God are not even being read or preached. No wonder we have not grasped the reality of an overcoming life. God purposed to bring His body on earth, THE CHURCH, into fullness and be overcomers in this world.

When you; "Hear what the Spirit says", the Bible becomes alive and it brings life. The Word brings light into every dark situation; the Word is God-breathed.

> **2 Pet 1:20** Knowing this first, that no prophecy of the scripture is of any private interpretation.
>
> **2 Pet 1:21** For the prophecy came not in old time by the will of man: but holy men of God spake [as they were] moved by the Holy Ghost.

Bible authors were inspired by the spirit, but no scripture can be of human interpretation.

> **1 Cor 2:14** But the natural man receiveth not the things of the Spirit of God: for they are foolishness unto him: neither can he know [them], because they are spiritually discerned.

> **John 6:63** It is the spirit that quickeneth; the flesh profiteth nothing: the words that I speak unto you… [they] are spirit, and [they] are life.

The Scripture explains itself, it is God breathed.

Isa 34:16 Seek ye out of the book of the LORD, and read: no one of
these shall fail, none shall want her mate: for my mouth it hath
commanded, and his spirit it hath gathered them.

• THE OLD SYSTEM OF WORSHIP

The mysteries locked up in the Word can only be revealed by the Spirit, at certain time periods ordained by God. The Bible uses terms like, "appointed time," "fullness of time" and even "designated time."

Eph 3:5 Which in other ages was not made known unto the sons of men,
as it is now revealed unto his holy apostles and prophets by the
Spirit;

There is a progression of revelation in the Word, and no book can be separated from the rest. The workings of God unfold as history develops. Foreshadowing is a very important principle that links the whole Bible from Genesis to Revelation and is often missed.

Death reigned from Adam to Moses, then a system of worship was added to harness death, but it was only a shadow of the true light, which was to come into the world. God's chosen people perverted this system and rejected the Christ, thus they chose darkness.

It took forty years to get Egypt out of the Israelites and it took forty years to remove the old system of worship. This was foreshadowing of what happened after the cross.

Jesus became the final sacrificial Lamb, but Israel went right on sacrificing, even though the veil was rent and there was no ark behind no veil anymore.

Heb 9:8 The Holy Ghost this signifying, that the way into the holiest of all was not yet made manifest, while as the first tabernacle was yet standing:

The old system was perverted and had to be removed. This process started when Israel was taken into captivity in Babylon. This degeneration of the system that was infiltrated with serpent seed, progressed from the captivity to Babylon, right through the period of the fullness of time, when the Christ was crucified, to the burning down of the temple in 70 AD, forty years later.

• GOD IS NOT THE AUTHOR OF CONFUSION

A good understanding of historical facts, symbolism, numbers and human traditions helps with understanding the Word and receiving revelation knowledge regarding the book of Revelation.

The disciples asked Jesus in Matthew chapter twenty-four as to when all these things would happen that He spoke to the Pharisees about, He answered; "Take heed that no man deceive you."

Ironically, most deception in the church world is about the so-called "End-Time Teaching." It looks as if Christians do not know whether they should come or go, run away or rather fly away. Scared to be left behind, they forget that the earth belongs to God and we are to rule and reign here.

Rev 5:10 And hast made us unto our God kings and priests: and we shall reign on the earth.

Incorrect interpretation of the Word, places us in the wrong time period and instead of possessing the Kingdom on earth, some people are waiting for doom and destruction, which was never meant for us, and our time.

The Devil has no more power and is not even able to condemn us, but he was a liar and deceiver from the beginning. He is the author of confusion so that we would miss the blessing of reading the book of Revelation, but God's purposes cannot be stopped.

Daniel also prophesied about our time.

> **Dan 7:18** But the saints of the most High shall take the kingdom, and possess the kingdom for ever, even for ever and ever.

We are to reign as kings and priests on the earth.
We are not to prepare for 'The End', or to fly away.

Every time there is some notable event, end time prophecies jump up like mushrooms, and when it does not come to pass, they do not even apologize. All end time predictions have failed, yet arrogantly, some people just do it all over again, and that for the gain of money. Why would you want money if you are to leave this planet, anyway?

The worst part is, that people believe it over and over again. It is now time that we know what the Bible teaches. God's Word does not change, it is forever settled in the heavens. God will not adapt to our traditions and teachings, we have to understand His plans.

• REVELATION IS NOT A BOOK TO FEAR

The entire book of Revelation can be divided into these five topics, namely:
1. Jesus Christ
2. The Church
3. The Adversary
4. The Countdown
5. The Kingdom

It is time that we embrace the message of the finished work of the Christ. The latter rain is yet to fall and creation is waiting for the manifestation of the Sons of God, those who know their identity in God, and who are not thrown of course by every wind of false doctrine. God is not going to hand the earth over to Satan, the loser.

The gospel had to be preached to the whole known world, where Israel was scattered around the Mediterranean Sea, by the four great world empires, Babylon, Medo-Persia, Greece, and Rome. When this was accomplished, God commanded John not to write down what was revealed and not to seal the visions, in order for us to understand and know the purposes of God. Do not let the devil deceive us through ignorance.

> **Rev 22:10** And he saith unto me, Seal not the sayings of the prophecy of this book: for the time is at hand.

• REVELATION IS A JOURNEY

Revelation is the finishing of the work that was started in the book of Genesis, accomplished on the Cross and completed in 70 AD. The old system was totally removed during this time and the earthly temple was destroyed, never to be rebuilt again. The book of Revelation reveals the victorious Rider on the white horse.

- On the cross, Jesus cried," IT IS FINISHED".
- In Revelation, the Spirit decrees, "IT IS DONE".

Understanding the book of Revelation leads you to discover your real destiny in God and entering into the wonderful Kingdom of God. We are to rule and reign in this life, right here and right now, on the earth. We are destined to be overcomers right now in this fallen state of creation.

My prayer is that this book will open the door of understanding the book of Revelation; that it will be a blessing in your walk with God, resulting in the fulfilling of God's purpose in and with your life.

Please note for the purposes of this book;
All Scriptures are from, the King James Version, the Amplified Version and the Message Bible.

TABLE OF CONTENTS

INTRODUCTION
TO BIBLICAL PRINCIPLES

Rev 1:1 (Amp)

[THIS IS] the revelation of Jesus Christ
[His unveiling of the divine mysteries]. God gave it to Him to disclose and make known to His bond-servant's certain things which must shortly and speedily come to pass in their entirety. And He sent and communicated it through His angel (messenger) to His bond-servant John,

The more I worked on this book: the more was being revealed to me and I cannot claim to know it all. I realize now, that the day we know it all, this imperfect realm we are in, will not be able to keep us bound.

May your understanding be enlightened through the simplicity of this book.

Revelation in the Word is progressive, and we cannot interpret the Word any other way than through the Spirit and the Word. The Book of Revelation is full of **keys** to unlock the mysteries that can only be revealed by the Spirit. These keys are also the connection to the entire book of Revelation. The mysteries of this awesome book of visions, will open up by using these keys. Word. Jesus is the Word, and He is the door. The Word is the Truth, and if you seriously take these points to heart, you will grow in knowledge and understanding of the Word.

The Greek word for revelation is apocalypses, and it means to reveal or to open up. God wants us to understand His workings and His Word. Gabriel was send to Daniel in order for him to understand and know the visions.

> *THAT IS WHY VISIONS, ARE VISIONS,*
> THEY ARE GIVEN SO THAT WE CAN KNOW THINGS
> AND NOT BE CONFUSED.

In the book Revelation, we find the cleaning up of the mess Satan caused for humanity. This led to a final destruction of the second world, the world of the law, with fire. '

> **2 Pet 3:6** Whereby the world that then was, being overflowed with water, perished:
> :7 But the heavens and the earth, which are now, by the same word are kept in store, reserved unto fire against the day of judgment and perdition of ungodly men.

• UNDERSTAND THE WORD

The book, in its totality, is all about the Word and the revealing of the redemption plan for man. If you do not see Jesus Christ on every page, you have not understood the purpose of the written Word.

> **Heb 10:7** Then said I, Lo, I come (in the volume of the book it is written of me,) to do thy will, O God.

The Word is unchangeable and is forever settled in the heavens. It is the biggest gift ever given to mankind. The Word was from the beginning and everything was made by it.

- **The Word brought light and life into darkness.**
- **The Word became flesh and dwelt among us.**

1 Tim 3:16 And without controversy great is the mystery of godliness: God was manifest in the flesh, justified in the Spirit, seen of angels, preached unto the Gentiles, believed on in the world, received up into glory.

- Jesus is the answer; He did not just bring it.
- Jesus is the way; He does not just open it.
- He is the truth; He does not just reveal it.
- Jesus is the Life: He did not just give it.
- He is the place prepared for us

The Word defines and explains itself, through the understanding given by the Spirit.

Isa 34:16 Seek ye out of the book of the LORD, and read: no one of these shall fail, none shall want her mate: for my mouth it hath commanded, and his spirit it hath gathered them.

• KNOW THE TOPIC

Four thousand years after the fall of man, John connects us back to the beginning. Through the principles of first mentioning, foreshadowing, foretelling and the prophetic, the entire bible is connected.

> **John 1:1** In the beginning was the Word, and the Word was with God, and the Word was God.
> :2 The same was in the beginning with God.
> :3 All things were made by him; and without him was not anything made that was made.
> :4 In him was life; and the life was the light of men.
> :5 And the light shineth in darkness; and the darkness comprehended it not.

JESUS IS THE LIGHT
JESUS IS THE CREATOR
JESUS IS THE WAY, THE TRUTH AND THE LIFE

John brings us right into God's plan on day four, the fullness of time. Day four is the middle of the week.

> **Gal 4:4** But when the fullness of the time was come, God sent forth his Son, made of a woman, made under the law.

John wrote the book of John, the epistles of John and Revelation. He was the only Apostle of the Lamb that lived beyond the final removal of the old system, in 70 AD.

> **Rev 1:9** I John, who also am your brother, and companion in tribulation, and in the kingdom and patience of Jesus Christ, was in the isle that is called Patmos, for the word of God, and for the testimony of Jesus Christ.

John announces that the true Light was coming into the world, right on schedule. Christ Himself brought us the Light Life, when the Word was made flesh and dwelt amongst us. He became the first spiritual man.

> **1 Cor 15:45** And so it is written, The first man Adam was made a living soul; the last Adam [was made] a quickening spirit.

• SPIRITUAL INSPIRATION

Spiritual inspiration comes from the spirit, the Creator Himself. To be inspired, is to be breathed upon by the Spirit, which results in having revelation. It is the living Word that brings light to every situation.

> **2 Pe 1:20** Knowing this first, that no prophecy of the scripture is of any private interpretation.
> :21 For the prophecy came not in old time by the will of man: but holy men of God spake as they were moved by the Holy Ghost.

God is Spirit and is timeless and omnipresent. He cannot be worshipped in the flesh, with the carnal mind. We need to learn how to conduct our earthly life, in the Spirit, the place prepared, right here on earth.

The way John received the visions is the only way we will ever understand them; by revelation through the Spirit. We need to hear what the Spirit says.

> **Rev 1:10** I was in the Spirit on the Lord's day, and heard behind
> me a great voice, as of a trumpet,

> **John 3:8** The wind bloweth where it listeth, and thou hearest
> the sound thereof, but canst not tell whence it cometh, and
> whither it goeth: so is every one that is born of the Spirit.

> **Rom 8:14** For as many as are led by the Spirit of God, they are the
> sons of God.

• UNDERSTAND BIBLE PATTERNS

• PROPHECIES

Prophecies in the Bible are for specific times and for specific groups of people. Wrong interpretation of prophesy leaves you lost and confused in the corridors of time and keeps you from ever reaching your destiny. Misplacing prophecy, causes sincere believers either to be imprisoned by a spirit of fear and without direction. It is like when someone is waiting for a bus that has long gone. It creates confusion and it paralyses purposes.

• THE PRINCIPLE OF FIRST MENTIONING

The first time something is mentioned in the word is always very important, for it sets the trend throughout the Bible. It is spiritual principles that link the Word throughout human history and helps us understand the unfolding of God's plan and connects Genesis to Revelation.

The principle of first mentioning sets the stage for what is to come. It foreshadows the real event. The tabernacle was a shadow of the heavenly things as well as, what was to come.

• THE PRINCIPLE OF FORESHADOWING

Foreshadowing is a major important key, it does not only link truths throughout the word, it reveals the future for those that have an ear for the Spirit. The Bible is the story of the battle for the right seed, taken from human history but inspired by the Spirit. There is a golden thread of connection in the Word.

THE WHOLE BIBLE IS PROPHETIC.
THE TESTIMONY OF JESUS
IS THE SPIRIT OF PROPHESY (REV 19:10).

The Spirit is a dimension that is not bound to time. Lessons can be taken from what happened in history and applied in your personal experience, though the happenings are not really relevant to our time period.

• THE WORD IS SPIRIT BREATHED

2 Tim 3:16 All scripture is given by inspiration of God, and
is profitable for doctrine, for reproof, for correction, for
instruction in righteousness:

Gal 3:8 And the scripture, foreseeing that God would justify
the heathen through faith, preached before the gospel unto
Abraham, [saying], In thee shall all nations be blessed

• UNDERSTAND TIME

Time is relative and works out in the natural, earthly environment.
God is Spirit and He describes time in a different way, it is more like a
concept of a specific period, than our minutes, hours, days and years.
A day to God can mean one day or a determined time period, or even
a life span.

2 Peter 3:8 But, beloved, be not ignorant of this one thing, that
one day is with the Lord as a thousand years, and a thousand
years as one day.

We know that God created everything in seven days, but we might
not understand clearly what we know. Unfortunately, there are too
many people caught up in arguments regarding the Scriptures,
without understanding the scriptures themselves. This may sound
strange, but if you do a study of Genesis one and two, it seems like
the Bible contradicts itself, but when you read the whole Word and
understand the Spirit of the Word, it makes perfect sense.

Gen 2:4 These [are] the generations of the heavens and of the
earth when they were created, in the day that the LORD God
made the earth and the heavens,

Seven days are called one generation, as well as a day. How do you
like that? These are not riddles. They are time periods set by God
and they can only be understood in the Spirit. It is God's spiritual
blueprint, for this age.
Moses wrote the book of Genesis, though he lived two thousand five
hundred years after Adam. He was totally inspired by the Spirit and
gave us the only record of creation, he also described his own death.

• THERE IS NO TIME IN THE SPIRIT

God's workings are revealed by the Spirit, through the scriptures.

Heb 11:3 Through faith we understand that the worlds were
framed by the word of God, so that things which are seen were
not made of things which do appear.

The creation week described in Genesis one, is also God's blueprint
for this age. These seven days cannot be taken as twenty-four-hour
days, because days, as we know it, were only created on day four.

Gen 1:14 And God said, Let there be lights in the firmament of
the heaven to divide the day from the night; and let them be
for signs, and for seasons, and for days, and years:
:15 And let them be for lights in the firmament of the heaven to

give light upon the earth: and it was so.

:16 And God made two great lights; the greater light to rule the day, and the lesser light to rule the night: [he made] the stars also.

:17 And God set them in the firmament of the heaven to give light upon the earth,

:18 And to rule over the day and over the night, and to divide the light from the darkness: and God saw that [it was] good.

:19 And the evening and the morning were the fourth day.

On Day One, God called light into existence and only on Day Four, He created the sun, moon and stars, which are the time clocks for humanity to determine days and nights.

God gave Adam a warning that they would die in the day that they eat of the forbidden tree. Did they die that day?

WHAT DAY?
GOD'S DAY, OR MAN'S DAY?

Deceived by Satan, they disobeyed and immediately they fell from the realm of fellowship with God and died spiritually. Man was never meant to die, but after the fall, no-one became older than a thousand years and after the flood, man's life span started to diminish down to one hundred and twenty years.

Moses complained to God that in the desert the people only became seventy and the strong ones eighty.

• TIME IS IN HIS HANDS

Rev 1:8 …the Lord, which is, and which was, and which is to come, the Almighty.

God does not have a beginning or an end; He is eternal. God is Spirit, He is ever in the present, the "Great I Am." He, alone has immortality. It is a place of perfection with no condemnation.

Rom 8:1 There, is therefore, now no condemnation to them which are in Christ Jesus, who walk not after the flesh, but after the Spirit.

Spirit is also a place, and is not bound to time. There is no past or future in the Spirit, there is only the present tense: NOW.

Too often "now" is missed in the Word.

2 Cor 6:2 NOW... is the accepted time; behold, NOW…is the day of salvation.

• THE FULLNESS OF TIME

On the first day God created light and only on the fourth day, He created the sun and the moon to form days and nights. Jesus came to this earth in the fullness of time.

The first chapter of John is filled with revelation of Jesus Christ and it announces a new beginning and links the word with the first beginning back in Genesis, over four-thousand years of history, right to the beginning. He announces that the "True Light" has now come into the earth to enlighten mankind, four thousand years after Adam. In revelation Jesus is introduced as the beginning and the end.

The fourth day forms the middle of the seven-day creation week and we know that it was in "The fullness of time", that God sent forth His SON. It was a new beginning, the end is always a new beginning in the spirit. This was the beginning of the generation of sons, the battle for seed is over.

> **John 1:1** In the beginning was the Word, and the Word was with God, and the Word was God.
> :2 The same was in the beginning with God.
> :3 All things were made by him; and without him was not anything made that was made.
> :4 In him was life; and the life was the light of men.
> :5 And the light shineth in darkness; and the darkness comprehended it not.

> **John 1:9** [That] was the true Light, which lighteth every man that cometh into the world.

> John 1:14 And the Word was made flesh, and dwelt among us, (and we beheld his glory, the glory as of the only begotten of the Father,) full of grace and truth.

• UNDERSTAND THE HISTORY SETTING

The battle for seed played out during the history of the human race and this story is recorded in the Word. History is often referred to as "His Story" working through generation after generation. God progressively reveals His plan and no man can change God's set times.

AS TIME GOES, REVELATION GROWS.

The "appointed time" and "fullness of time", are terms generally used throughout Scripture, and we cannot alter God's appointed times. We can only study and understand them.

For forty years the Israelites wandered through the desert because of their disobedience. You can, in no way, change that.

> **Num 14:34** After the number of the days in which ye searched the land, even forty days, each day for a year, shall ye bear your iniquities, even forty years, and ye shall know my breach of promise.

In the same way, it took forty years to get rid of that wicked generation from the cross to the burning of the temple, removing the old and bringing in the new.

We can only interpret the time, not determine or change time.

• UNDERSTAND THE SPIRIT OF BABYLON

Babel means confusion. Right after the flood, the people attempted to build a tower, trying to reach God and be like Him. God called it Babel, meaning confusion. God himself intervened and stopped them, but this story is repeated over and over in history, in empires and individuals lives. Satan himself is the spirit behind Babylon, and his main mission is, and has always been to corrupt God's seed.

God called and built himself a nation, but they kept disobeying God, till He gave them over and sent them to Babylon, in order for their eyes to open.

> **Isa 43:14** Thus saith the LORD, your redeemer, the Holy One of Israel; For your sake I have sent to Babylon,

Instead of repenting, they started their own religion and sinned themselves bankrupt. Their final downfall and removal started in Babylon, and in Revelation seventeen, they resembled Babylon in the form of a whore, drunk with the blood of martyrs and prophets and Babylon written on her forehead. This was prophesied by Isaiah.

> **Isa 1:21** How is the faithful city become an harlot! it was full of judgment; righteousness lodged in it; but now murderers.

Judah's captivity in Babylon marked the beginning of Israel's downfall.
God's prophets have warned His people of the wrath to come, but they killed the prophets and the Son, continuing the course of their

final destruction, in 70AD.

The New Testament plays out in a very important specific portion of history. Rome ruled the world during this time, and Rome was the last world empire that ruled in succession, according to Nebuchadnezzar's dream and that reveals the specific time period.

In **Dan 7:7,** Daniel also dreamed of these four empires from Dan 2, but now they were in the form of animals.

1. Head = Babylon = Lion
2. Breast = Medo - Persia = Bear
3. Thighs = Greece = Leopard
4. Legs = Rome = Vicious animal

In a body, the head is where the direction comes from, so the spirit behind Rome was Babylon. The whole known world was prepared for the coming of the Christ, also called the fullness of time.

Rome built roads that linked places and that lead to the mingling of all the cultures and a universal language and this culture is studied intensively.

Yet it amazed me how little is known about the history during and after the crucifixion. The only sources of information on what really happened from the Cross right up to 70 AD, is; The Bible, Josephus's writings and Roman history.

Jesus was born, died and rose again, during the time of the Roman

Empire, a direct link to Babylon.

The book of Revelation is also written during Roman Rulership. The end of Judaism started with the captivity to Babylon, followed by the four-hundred years of silence, and ended in 70 AD., forty years after their rejection of their Messiah.

• THE DAY OF VENGEANCE

Jesus came to His own people, but they rejected Him. They not only rejected him First they tried to take the kingdom by force trying to be baptized without repenting.

> **Luke 3:7** Then said he to the multitude that came forth to be baptized of him, O generation of vipers, who hath warned you to flee from the wrath to come?
> :8 Bring forth therefore fruits worthy of repentance, and begin not to say within yourselves, We have Abraham to our father: for I say unto you, That God is able of these stones to raise up children unto Abraham.
> :9 And now also the axe is laid unto the root of the trees: every tree therefore which bringeth not forth good fruit is hewn down, and cast into the fire.

Instead of repenting, they allied with Rome plotting His death and thus releasing the wrath of God on themselves, fulfilling all the prophecies of about that wicked generation. The minute the Lamb of God was slaughtered, the seals of Daniel's visions were broken, and God's wrath was poured on that generation, who rejected their

King and called for his blood on them and their children. This was all prophesied by Moses.

> **Deut 32:35** To me [belongeth] vengeance, and recompense; their foot shall slide in [due] time: for the day of their calamity [is] at hand, and the things that shall come upon them make haste.

The Word explains the Word, and important points automatically connect. The same angel that appeared to Daniel also announced the birth of both John and Jesus. Jesus also refers to Daniel when He was explaining the time of the end of that world, the law world. In Matthew twenty-four, Jesus described this time period to His disciples.

The Day of Vengeance was prophesied to them and they actually tried to escape it by trying to be baptized. They knew all about it.

> **Luke 3:7** Then said he to the multitude that came forth to be baptized of him, O generation of vipers, who hath warned you to flee from the wrath to come?

> **Isa 13:6** Howl ye; for the day of the LORD [is] at hand; it shall come as a destruction from the Almighty.

> **Mal 4:5** Behold, I will send you Elijah the prophet before the coming of the great and dreadful day of the LORD:

> **Joel 1:15** Alas for the day! for the day of the LORD [is] at hand, and as a destruction from the Almighty shall it come.

> **Amos 5:18** Woe unto you that desire the day of the LORD! to

what end [is] it for you? the day of the LORD [is] darkness, and
   not light.

Zeph 1:7 Hold thy peace at the presence of the Lord GOD: for the
   day of the LORD [is] at hand: for the LORD hath prepared a
   sacrifice, he hath bid his guests.

Jer 46:10 For this [is] the day of the Lord GOD of hosts, a day of
   vengeance, that he may avenge him of his adversaries: and the
   sword shall devour, and it shall be satiate and made drunk
   with their blood:

Jer 51:6 Flee out of the midst of Babylon, and deliver every man
   his soul: be not cut off in her iniquity; for this [is] the time of
   the LORD'S vengeance; he will render unto her a recompense.
It is shocking to see how many times this day was prophesied.

The day of Vengeance is a time period of the final removal of the
old and is described in the book of Revelation from chapter six up
to chapter twenty. It was the, "Day of Vengeance", that came like, "A
Thieve in the Knight", of which the prophets and Moses warned Israel
about.

Jesus referred to this time in Matthew twenty-four and it correlates
with the visions of Daniel. It was the time of, "Great Tribulation", as
was never seen before.

The Day, was the thief, God is not and will never be a thief. The
DAY of Vengeance is the period that the old system of worship was
removed and Chapter four deals with it.

• THE END OF THE WORLD

Heb 1:10 And, Thou, Lord, in the beginning hast laid the foundation of the earth; and the heavens are the works of thine hands:

Heb 4:3 For we which have believed do enter into rest, as he said, As I have sworn in my wrath, if they shall enter into my rest: although the works were finished from the foundation of the world.

Jesus died and was crucified before the foundation of the world, NOT THE EARTH, and at the end at the end of the world, it took place. This was promised to Abraham four-hundred and thirty years before and revealed to Moses, who was commanded to bring the system of worship in order.

Heb 9:26 For then must he often have suffered since the foundation of the world: but now once in the end of the world hath he appeared to put away sin by the sacrifice of himself.

Rev 13:8 And all that dwell upon the earth shall worship him, whose names are not written in the book of life of the Lamb slain from the foundation of the world.

We read about the rulers of the world. That crucified the Christ. They worshipped the system instead of worshipping God, who gave them the system. The system had to be removed, because it was abused and it blocked the manifestation of the very thing it was supposed to do?

Heb 9:8 The Holy Ghost this signifying, that the way into the holiest of all was not yet made manifest, while as the first tabernacle was yet standing:

In Matthew twenty-four, Jesus departed from the temple for the last time and mentioned that not one stone would be left upon another. The disciples then asked Jesus a three-fold question:

Matt 24:3 And as he sat upon the mount of Olives, the disciples came unto him privately, saying, Tell us,

1. When shall these things be? and
2. What [shall be] the sign of thy coming? and
3. When of the end of the world?

Jesus' answer is yet to be understood, even today, because most of the deception going around in the church world, concerns the understanding of end of the world.

Matt 24:4 And Jesus answered and said unto them, Take heed that no man deceive you.

Jesus then explained how the beginning of sorrows and the time of sorrows would be.

Matt 24:6 And ye shall hear of wars and rumours of wars: see that ye be not troubled: for all [these things] must come to pass, but the end is not yet.

Matt 24:7 For nation shall rise against nation, and kingdom against kingdom: and there shall be famines, and pestilences,

and earthquakes, in divers places.
:8 All these [are] the beginning of sorrows.

Matt 24:14 And this gospel of the kingdom shall be preached in all the world for a witness unto all nations; and then shall the end come.

The end of the forty-years that followed the Crucifixion was described in Daniel twelve; "and there shall be a time of trouble (Amplified version- tribulation), such as never was since there was a nation [even] to that same time:"

This is what the end in the World is all about, not the earth.
Jesus died at the end of the Law world.

Heb 9:26 For then must he often have suffered since the foundation of the world: but now once in the end of the world hath he appeared to put away sin by the sacrifice of himself.

The book of Peter describes two worlds, one that was already destroyed, and one was about to be destroyed, and that by the two life giving elements; water and fire.

2 Pet 3:6 Whereby the world that then was, being overflowed with water, perished:
:7 But the heavens and the earth, which are now, by the same word are kept in store, reserved unto fire against the day of judgment and perdition of ungodly men.

The first world was destroyed because of sin that abounded, and God regretted ever making man. Noah and eight souls were saved by the ark through water, but the sin that controlled man came through the ark with them, and we know death reigned from Adam to Moses.

In Moses God installed a system to harness sin while preparing creation for the fullness of time and the coming Christ. They had to prepare an ark with the Testimonies inside, the schoolmaster to Christ. The whole tabernacle was a shadow of the things in heaven and foreshadowed the good things to come on the earth. (Heb 8, 9 & 10).

Infiltrated by Satan's seed, they became a brood of vipers, an abomination to God.

> **Jer 2:7** And I brought you into a plentiful country, to eat the fruit ,thereof and the goodness thereof; but when ye entered, ye defiled my land, and made mine heritage an abomination.

Christ was the end of the LAW WORLD and 70 A.D. was the total removal of that world. The book of revelation describes this whole process that took forty years, from the cross to 70 A.D.

> **Rom 10:4** For Christ [is] the end of the law for righteousness to everyone that believeth.

- UNDERSTAND NUMBERS

- THE FORTY CONCEPT

Forty is a set time that resembles a generation on earth.

    4 = earthy

    10 = complete

    40 = a generation, the time it takes to bring in the new.

These principles are found throughout Bible history.

- Forty days of rain in Noah's time destroying the first world.
- Forty years Israel wandered through the desert before entering.
- Forty days Ezekiel lay on his side, predicting the forty years
- Nineveh was to be overthrown in forty days, yet they repented.

JESUS DIED IN JERUSALEM 30 AD
THE TEMPLE WAS BURNED DOWN 70 AD.

The forty years after the cross is a period of refining and removal of the old, in order for the new to be established. John was the only apostle alive. He lived through the time of transition from tribulation to the kingdom.

> **Rev 1:9** I John, who also am your brother, and companion in tribulation, and in the kingdom and patience of Jesus Christ, was in the isle that is called Patmos, for the Word of God, and for the testimony of Jesus Christ.

Jesus came first and foremost to Israel and the Gospel had to be preached to them first. He gave them three and a half years, yet without any fruit, and trees had to be cut down and burned. John announced that the axe is already at the roots, yet they were given another three and a half years.

There were many Jews that did not even know about what happened in Jerusalem for they were scattered around the Mediterranean during all the wars around Jerusalem since Babylon. The kingdom came, but the gospel had to be preached to all these Jews first, before the inauguration, of the kingdom.

> **Matt 24:14** And this gospel of the kingdom shall be preached in all the world for a witness unto all nations; and then shall the end come.

THE END OF THE LAW WORLD, NOT THE EARTH.

> **Rev 15:8** And the temple was filled with smoke from the glory of God, and from his power; and no man was able to enter into the temple, till the seven plagues of the seven angels were fulfilled.

> **Matt 24:34** Verily I say unto you, This generation shall not pass, till all these things be fulfilled.

God gave Israel yet another chance to turn to God, but they would not.

> **Acts 13:46** Then Paul and Barnabas waxed bold, and said, It was necessary that the Word of God should first have been spoken to you: but seeing ye put it from you, and judge yourselves unworthy of everlasting life, lo, we turn to the Gentiles.

The rulers of the temple persecuted the Christians to a point where it aggravated Rome, who now turned on the Jews. In 66 AD, Rome surrounded Jerusalem, until they totally destroyed the city and burned the temple, in 70AD.

This marked the finishing of the work of the Son of Man, who ruled them with a Rod of Iron(Rome), and the total removal of the old, the system that was a schoolmaster to Christ. Ezekiel also prophesied about this forty-year period, that would come upon Israel.

> **Ezek 4:6** … lie again on thy right side, and thou shalt bear the iniquity of the house of Judah forty days: I have appointed thee each day for a year.
> **:7** Therefore thou shalt set thy face toward the siege of Jerusalem, and thine arm [shall be] uncovered, and thou shalt prophesy against it.

Jesus described this period in Matthew twenty-four and Luke thirteen clearly as the coming of the SON OF MAN, to finish what was started on the cross.

> **Matt 23:36** Verily I say unto you, All these things shall come upon this generation. (a generation is forty years)

• SEVEN; GOD OF HEAVEN AND EARTH

Israel perverted the system of worship and refused to keep the seventh Sabbath year when the land had to rest. This was preparing for the year of Jubilee, every fiftieth year. After seven of Sabbath years, it was the year of Jubilee and it was a year of restoration and debt cancellation and freedom to the people.

Israel did not respect God's command and did not follow the pattern set and then were now taken to Babylon for seventy years.

7 = 3+4 = God working with Earth

10 = Complete

70 = a complete time period

God gave them a complete time, seventy years to repent, but instead, they created their own system of worship within the law, and they instituted Sadducees, Pharisees, and Synagogues. This was never God's intention. They now resemble the fig tree, remember the fig leaves in the garden. Fig meaning; "I will do it my way".

Matt 23:1 Then spake Jesus to the multitude, and to his disciples, :2 Saying, The scribes and the Pharisees sit in Moses' seat:

Matt 21:19 And when he saw a fig tree in the way, he came to it, and found nothing thereon, but leaves only, and said unto it, Let no fruit grow on thee henceforward for ever. And presently the fig tree withered away.

Israel ignored God's warnings and killed the prophets that were sent to them, thus becoming an abomination to God. They perverted the whole system of worship, and in Revelation it is clear that God now rejected them.

Rev 2:9 I know thy works, and tribulation, and poverty, (but thou art rich) and [I know] the blasphemy of them which say they are Jews, and are not, but [are] the synagogue of Satan.

Daniel arrived in Babylon at about the age of sixteen. Israel spent 70 years in captivity in Babylon and at the end of seventy years in captivity, he read out of the book of Jeremiah and realized the significance of the time he found himself in and started interceding for his people.

The angel Gabriel unveiled the future to Daniel and revealed a time period of 70x7, 490 years, that would lead up to the coming of their Messiah. This period is also known as the four-hundred years of silence. Daniel ten and eleven, reveals the history that played out during this time. Gabriel also described a terrible time of tribulation and distress that was to befall Daniel's people and their city, after the 70x7 years.
Daniel was commanded to seal those visions, for it was meant for another period when it would be opened and understood.

Dan 12:4 But thou, O Daniel, shut up the words, and seal the book, [even] to the time of the end: many shall run to and fro, and knowledge shall be increased.

Dan 12:9 And he said, Go thy way, Daniel: for the words [are] closed up and sealed till the time of the end.

Understanding the spiritual language, brings new life and light to the Word. A good example is found in Matthew eighteen. The Apostle

Peter asked Jesus about forgiveness;

Matt 18:21 Then came Peter to him, and said, Lord, how often shall my brother sin against me, and I forgive him? till seven times?

:22 Jesus saith unto him, I say not unto thee, Until seven times: but, Until seventy times seven.

In the answer, Jesus actually told Peter that they had no concept of what God actually did for them.

In Revelation four, the time has finally arrived for the Kingdom to be established. The things concerning Jesus has ended, but the Spirit, the Christ abides forever.

1 Tim 3:16 And without controversy great is the mystery of godliness: God was manifest in the flesh, justified in the Spirit, seen of angels, preached unto the Gentiles, believed on in the world, received up into glory.

Luk 22:37 For I say unto you, that this that is written must yet be accomplished in me, And he was reckoned among the transgressors: for the things concerning me have an end.

John 12:34 The people answered him, We have heard out of the law that Christ abideth for ever: and how sayest thou, The Son of man must be lifted up? who is this Son of man?

• NUMBERS AS SYMBOLS

Every number has significance and their combinations tell a story and we can understand the inspiration of the Spirit in the Word. All numbers are a combination of 1, 2 and 3

1 = Unity

2 = Agreement

3 = The number for God, Father, Son and Holy Ghost

4 = The number for creation; can mean earth or earthy
 North, South, East, and West

5 = Grace and spiritual ministry

6 = The number of man

666 = 3 x 6   Man trying to elevate himself to God

7 = 3 + 4 Heaven and earth, God working with man
 Seven spirits, Seven seals, Seven vials,

12 = 3 x 4   God's governing number,
 Twelve tribes, Twelve apostles

24 = 12 + 12 = (3x4) + (3x4) = elders in heaven
 Twelve in the New and twelve in the Old

144000 = 12 x 12 x 1000 All God's people throughout all ages.

10 = The number for completion

7 x 10 = 70   Complete time

3 x 1o = 30   Maturity

4 x 10 = 40   A Generation

1000 = 10x10x10 = Perfection

If you know number symbols this next verse is packed with revelation.

Rev 9:15 And the four angels were loosed, which were prepared for an hour, and a day, and a month, and a year, for to slay the third part of men.

• THE SYMBOLIC LANGUAGE OF THE BIBLE

In the four gospels, we read the words, "it was fulfilled", this ties the Word together. Symbols in the Old Testament must then correspond with symbols in the New Testament. We have to read the Word as a whole and seek the mates and find their fulfilment.

Isa 34:16 Seek ye out of the book of the LORD, and read: no one of these shall fail, none shall want her mate: for my mouth it hath commanded, and his spirit it hath gathered them.

Trying to take everything literally and not understanding the symbolic meanings will leave you lost in the natural world, in utter confusion. Here is a good example:

Rev 11:8 And their dead bodies [will lie exposed] in the open street (a public square) of the great city which is in a spiritual sense called [by the mystical and allegorical names of] Sodom and Egypt, where also their Lord was crucified.

If you have read and understood the book of Deuteronomy chapters twenty-nine to thirty-two, then this Scripture would be no problem. God told Moses to sing Israel a song about what their latter –end be like. They were a disobedient hard necked people that sinned themselves bankrupt, and that they would become like the vine of Sodom and finally be destroyed by fire. I do not know how you sing a song like that.

They became an abomination unto God and in Revelation, this came in to fulfilment.

> **Rev 15:3** And they sing the song of Moses the servant of God, and the song of the Lamb, saying, Great and marvellous [are] thy works, Lord God Almighty; just and true [are] thy ways, thou King of saints.

• SYMBOLS

The symbolic is the language of the Spirit and is very important. In this book I concentrate more on numbers, but understanding symbols opens things in another direction, for every colour, number, and object has a meaning.

Here are a few keys.
  - Angel- Messenger
  - Armageddon- High place of decision.
  - Babylon/Egypt/Sodom- Israel became what they worshipped
  - Iron- Rome (the rod of persecution)

- Beast- The forces of evil, the systems of the world
- Dragon- Power of evil, Satan
- False prophet- The woman Israel infiltrated with serpent seed
- Horns- Kings
- Heads- Rulers
- Jezebel- Rejecting authority
- East- Source of life, place of paradise, firstly
- Eyes, The all-seeing, all-knowing power of God
- Lamp stands- The Church, Christ's body on earth
- New Jerusalem- Where Christ has supreme authority
- Virgins- People who never indulged in any idolatrous practices
- Red Horse- A bloody war (Huge sword=violence)
- White Horse- A conquering power (Bow=oppression)
- Black Horse- Famine
- Scale - shortage of food with increase of price
- Pale Horse- Death and Decay (Hades=Netherworlds)
- Sword- God's Spoken Word
- Trumpet- God's voice
- Seven Trumpets - Persecution by Rome on the city
- Seven Seals - Visions sealed by Daniel
- Seven Vials- Final last plagues on the earthly temple
- Lamb- Crucified Christ
- Lion of the Tribe of Judah- The glorified Christ
- Eagle – Power, and swiftness of divine help
- Woman- Israel bringing forth the Messiah
- Stars- 12 Tribes
- Sun, moon, and stars- The house of Israel
- Lion, Eagle, Calf, Man- God manifested in flesh
- Sea- Source of evil, where beast comes from
- Scroll- Gods' purpose for creation
- The Lord's Day- Day of vengeance

It is now time to actually go into the book. I pray that the understanding of the book will help you understand the finished work of Christ on the cross and how it effects this resurrection life working inside of us, taking us towards perfection.

Jesus Christ
CHAPTER ONE:

1 Tim 3:16
And without controversy great is the mystery of godliness:
God was manifest in the flesh, justified in the Spirit,
seen of angels, preached unto the Gentiles,
believed on in the world, received up into glory.

Jesus was the total fulfilment of the law and the prophets. The biggest event ever to happen on the earth was when God revealed himself to mankind, after man rejected everything that God freely gave them in Paradise.

We need a fresh revelation of JESUS, the CHRIST and present Him to the world for who he really was, GOD MANIFESTED IN FLESH.

My father was a famous artist, and I know a good picture when I see one. My biggest frustration in life has always been when people show me pictures that are totally rubbish. I do not even want to look at it, I'd rather look away. This is exactly how I feel about Satan; he is a bad picture. Why should we even be bothered about him. Hebrews twelve is a good instruction for life.

> **Heb 12:2** (Ampl) Looking away [from all that will distract] (look) to Jesus, Who is the Leader and the Source of our faith [giving the first incentive for our belief] and is also its Finisher [bringing it to maturity and perfection]. He, for the joy [of

obtaining the prize] that was set before Him, endured the cross, despising and ignoring the shame, and is now seated at the right hand of the throne of God.

Everything exists because of Christ and from Christ. He was the Word, that was from the beginning, and the same Word was made flesh to condemn sin in the flesh.

In the flesh the Living Word relied on the Written Word, when He was tested to deny God's Unchangeable Word and proved himself to be the Everlasting, Eternal Word.

The Bible, the written Word, contains the redemption plan worked out in human history, it is all about this living Word, that was being prepared to come into this world. Just the fact that Jesus came to this world, is enough proof of how much God loves His creation, and you are part of it.

> **John 3:16** For God so loved the world, that he gave his only begotten Son, that whosoever believeth in him should not perish, but have everlasting life.

The value of understanding the book of Revelation is unmeasurable, because it is the last and final book and it describes the completion of the redemption plan, the work started on the cross and was completed in 70 A.D. It is the completion of what was started in the beginning and the purposes of the Word, revealed. The biggest key to understanding the book of Revelation is found in chapter one, verse One;

Rev 1:1 The Revelation of Jesus Christ, which God gave…

It is all about JESUS CHRIST, the Author and Finisher of our faith *(Hebrews 12:3)*.

> **John 4:34** … My meat is to do the will of him that sent me and to finish his work.

> **1 John 3:8** … For this purpose, the Son of God was manifested, that he might destroy the works of the devil.

On the Cross, Jesus cried, "It is finished."

> **John 19:30** When Jesus, therefore had received the vinegar, he said, "It is finished":and he bowed his head, and gave up the ghost.

Forty years after the cross, on the isle of Patmos, He appeared to John and commanded him to write;

> **Rev 21:6** "It is done.". I am Alpha and Omega, the beginning and the end".

Please take note. It is not the book of Revelations, but Revelation; singular. Revelation actually has one subject, is all about; JESUS CHRIST, the Son of man, Son of God, the Victorious one. It is a revelation of the Christ and His work accomplished on the earth, for His bride, the church.

We are the object of His Love, this was all done for us.

Jesus Christ will not return for his church as the son of man, but as the Victorious Lord of Glory, for an overcoming Church, His Bride. He will not come as a thief; God is not and will never be a thief. His coming will be announced with a trumpet.

The day of the Lord was like a thief and came on that wicket generation that crucified their Messiah. They actually tried to escape Gods wrath by trying to be baptized by John.

2 Pe 3:10 But the day of the Lord will come as a thief in the night;
Mal 4:5 Behold, I will send you Elijah the prophet before the coming of the great and dreadful day of the LORD:

It is of utmost importance to understand this book. It is not a revelation about the beast, and the Anti-Christ is not even mentioned in this book, it is about the Christ and bringing creation back to their Creator.

In our day and age, the name of Jesus Christ has been watered down to a swearword. Jesus has become no more than a character found in a children's Bible. It seems that we have somehow lost the reality of Who the Lord Jesus Christ really is, yet at His Name, every knee shall bow.

> **Col 1:16** For it was in Him that all things were created, in heaven and on earth, things seen and things unseen, whether thrones, dominions, rulers, or authorities; all things were created and exist through Him [by His service, intervention] and in and for Him.
>
> :17 And He Himself existed before all things, and in Him all things consist (cohere, are held together).

Hebrews ten handles the failure of the sacrificial system that cannot free the conscience of man. Instead of removing the guilt, man is reminded of his fallen state year after year. Between it all the full redemption plan is also revealed.

> **Heb 10:7** Then said I, Lo, I come (in the volume of the book it is written of me,) to do thy will, O God.

> **Heb 10:5** Wherefore when he cometh into the world, he saith, Sacrifice and offering thou wouldest not, but a body hast thou prepared me:

> **Heb 10:9** Then said he, Lo, I come to do thy will, O God. He taketh away the first, that he may establish the second.

Revelation is the final removal of the old and the disclosure of the battle that was ignited in the garden between the two seeds, after Adam sold creation out to Satan. God, however, never intended to forsake His creation.

The Bible consists of sixty-six books but it is all about one topic; "GOD'S REDEMPTION PLAN FOR ALL OF MANKIND." There is a golden thread of life that runs through the entire book, and in Revelation we find the climax of the Word, describing the climax of the ages.

• THE SEED OF GOD

> **Gen 17:7** And I will establish my covenant between me and thee and thy seed after thee in their generations for an everlasting covenant, to be a God unto thee, and to thy seed after thee.

> **Gen 17:8** And I will give unto thee, and to thy seed after thee, the land wherein thou art a stranger, all the land of Canaan, for an everlasting possession; and I will be their God.

Here we find a covenant made between God and Abraham that is a generational seed line, but there was also mention of a single seed, the guarantee God has put in place. The generational seed line was totally contaminated by Satan himself and they became responsible for the death of Christ, who was God's guarantee for us to receive his promises.

GOD WHO SITS IN THE HEAVENS LAUGHS. (PS 2)

> **Gal 3:16** Now to Abraham and his seed were the promises made. He saith not, And to seeds, as of many; but as of one, And to thy seed, which is Christ.

Revelation describes the finale, this battle between the seeds, the battle between good and evil, which was ignited when Adam sold creation to Satan. Creation seemed doomed, but the battle was reduced to a single combat between the seed of the serpent and the seed of the woman. We know woman do not carry seed, but God himself overshadowed Mary, and took on the fight in our stead.

Throughout all the ages, Satan worked at contaminating the seed line of the sons of God, to prevent the Christ from coming. Twice he had a whole generation of babies killed and then he even tried to infiltrate even the woman that was to bring forth the Man Child.

NO MATTER WHAT SATAN DID, HE COULD NOT STOP GOD FROM RESTORING HIS CREATION. SATAN NEVER WAS, AND NEVER WILL BE, A MATCH FOR GOD.

As a baby Jesus was brought to the temple and he was recognized as the promised messiah. On entering that same temple, thirty years later, after being filled with the Spirit, Jesus called the Pharisees and Sadducees "Serpent Seed" and "Vipers."

The moment the Lamb was slain, the seals were broken and the four horses were revealed, the four winds that blew all over the world. This all started with the captivity of Israel to Babylon, igniting the downfall and removal of a system of worship that was distorted.

> **Dan 7:2** Daniel spake and said, I saw in my vision by night, and, behold, the four winds of the heaven strove upon the great sea.

:3 And four great beasts came up from the sea, diverse one from
    another.

The crucifixion ignited the "Day of Vengeance" and brought the
wrath of God down on that wicked generation, that called for the
blood of Christ upon them and their children.

1 Cor 2:7 But we speak the wisdom of God in a mystery, [even]
    the hidden [wisdom], which God ordained before the world
    unto our glory:
:8 Which none of the princes of this world knew: for had they
    known [it], they would not have crucified the Lord of glory.

Prophecies are the foreshadowing of the mysteries of God that were
progressively being revealed through time and the time now finally
came for their fulfilment.

Rev 10:6 And sware by him that liveth for ever and ever, who
    created heaven, and the things that therein are, and the earth,
    and the things that therein are, and the sea, and the things
    which are therein, that there should be time no longer:
:7 But in the days of the voice of the seventh angel, when he shall
    begin to sound, the mystery of God should be finished, as he
    hath declared to his servants the prophets.

• JESUS, THE FACE OF GOD

In Adam, all have sinned and come short of the Glory of God. Death
reigned from Adam to Moses. Two thousand five hundred years later,
God met Moses as a friend and spoke face to face with Him. (Ex 33 :11)

Moses requested to see God's glory, but God told Moses that He could not see God's face. However, God put Moses in the cleft of the rock beside Him and revealed His back parts to Moses. Back parts is the Greek word; "hawthorn" meaning; a rear point in time.

Moses in the spirit, saw the creation event in a split second. Thus he could write about the creation, he saw it in a vision. God revealed his Way to Moses, and it was Goodness, Mercy and Grace. Moses then had to cover His face because of the Glory that was fading. The end of that which is abolished.

> **2 Cor 3:14** But their minds were blinded: for until this day remaineth the same vail untaken away in the reading of the old testament; which [vail] is done away in Christ.
> :15 But even unto this day, when Moses is read, the vail is upon their heart.
> :16 Nevertheless when it shall turn to the Lord, the vail shall be taken away.
> :17 Now the Lord is that Spirit: and where the Spirit of the Lord [is], there [is] liberty.
> :18 But we all, with open face beholding as in a glass the glory of the Lord, are changed into the same image from glory to glory, [even] as by the Spirit of the Lord.

Jesus Christ is the Face of God, the glory that Moses was not able to see at that time.

> **2 Cor 4:6** For God, who commanded the light to shine out of darkness, hath shined in our hearts, to [give] the light of the

knowledge of the glory of God in the face of Jesus Christ.

• JESUS CHRIST REVEALED IN REVELATION ONE

The first chapter of Revelation paints a very clear and unmistakeable picture of who Jesus, the ultimate victorious One, is. This chapter really brings the whole Bible in perspective. Every verse, in chapter one could be a book on its own.

• HE IS THE FAITHFUL WITNESS (REV 1:5)

Acts 14:17 Nevertheless he left not himself without witness, in that he did good, and gave us rain from heaven, and fruitful seasons, filling our hearts with food and gladness.

Every time I read Hosea six, I cannot but feel overwhelmed by God's love.

Hos 6:3 Then shall we know, [if] we follow on to know the LORD: his going forth is prepared as the morning; and he shall come unto us as the rain, as the latter [and] former rain unto the earth.

Firstly; The heavens and the earth are forever a witness of His indescribable, Glory. On earth there is a progression in the revelation of the witnesses of God revealing Himself to man.

Everything in the Word is connected, for everything is about the Word. Jesus is the Faithful Witness, the Word revealed from the book of Genesis to the book of Revelation. He has been there since the beginning and all things existed by and through Him.

The volume of the book is about Him (Heb 10:7)
- In the beginning was the Word (John 1:1)
- He was the Rock that followed (1 Cor 10:4)
- He was the pattern of the whole tabernacle (Heb 8)
- The Word was made flesh (John 1:14)
- Christ is all and in all (Acts 17:28)
- Son of God, Son of Man amongst the candlesticks (Rev 1:13)
- He is the Rider on the White Horse (Rev 19)
- Jesus Christ the same yesterday, today and forever(Heb 13:8)
-He is, and was, and is to come, the Almighty (Rev 1:8)

Jesus, the faithful witness is revealed in three stages, yet He is ever in the present, the great, "I AM". He was, "I AM", He is, "I Am", and will be forever, "I AM". Times change, but God never changes.

THE SPIRIT IS NOT BOUND TO TIME.
IN THE SPIRIT ALL AGES AND LEVELS COME TOGETHER.

1. The law and the prophets witnessed until John.
   John was not the light; he was a witness to the light.
2. The Father himself witnessed about the Son.
   The works Jesus did, witnessed about His Glory.
3. The Spirit remaining on Him, witnessed of His Sonship.

The disciples became the witnesses, being filled with the Spirit. Now, the Spirit and the Bride carries the witness.

• WAS, IS AND IS TO COME

God is in the ever present, but we operate in time, which is divided in past, present, and future. In Revelation it is described in the spirit as; WAS, IS and IS TO COME. The Bible is also divided into three periods and Christ is forever the Faithful Witness;

WAS – Old Testament; Witnessed by Law and prophets (Matt 11:13)
IS - Christ's ministry; Witnessed by Father and Son (John 8:18)
IS TO COME - After the Cross; The Spirit and the Bride (Acts 1:8)

We are now in the, "IS TO COME" time frame, and this time is divided into two periods, the former rain and the former and the latter rain, prophesied by the prophet Joel.

> **Joel 2:23** Be glad then, ye children of Zion, and rejoice in the LORD your God: for he hath given you the former rain moderately, and he will cause to come down for you the rain, the former rain, and the latter rain in the first [month].(IN ONE)

Rain resembles the way that God cares and provides. It comes down from heaven to earth, bringing new life.

> **Isa 55:10** For as the rain cometh down, … :11 So shall my word

be that goeth forth out of my mouth: it shall not return unto me void, but it shall accomplish that which I please, and it shall prosper [in the thing] whereto I sent it.

The falling of the former rain was confirmed by Peter at Pentecost.

Acts 2:16 But this is that which was spoken by the prophet Joel;
:17 And it shall come to pass in the last days, saith God, I will pour out of my Spirit upon all flesh: and your sons and your daughters shall prophesy, and your young men shall see visions, and your old men shall dream dreams:

THE LATTER RAIN IS YET TO BE FULFILLED, BUT IS FORESHADOWED IN ACTS.

Acts 3:19 Repent ye therefore, and be converted, that your sins may be blotted out, when the times of refreshing shall come from the presence of the Lord;
:20 And he shall send Jesus Christ, which before was preached unto you:
:21 Whom the heaven must receive until the times of restitution of all things, which God hath spoken by the mouth of all his holy prophets since the world began.

This started around the 1900's when outpourings, restoration, of the Spirit occurring spontaneously, but creation is still groaning in anticipation for the full effect of the Spirit.

James 5:7 Be patient therefore, brethren, unto the coming of the Lord. Behold, the husbandman waited for the precious fruit of the earth, and hath long patience for it, until he receives the early and latter rain.

Zech 10:1 Ask ye of the LORD rain in the time of the latter rain; [so] the LORD shall make bright clouds, and give them showers of rain, to every one grass in the field.

Hos 6:2 After two days will he revive us: in the third day he will raise us up, and we shall live in his sight.
:3 Then shall we know, [if] we follow on to know the LORD: his going forth is prepared as the morning; and he shall come unto us as the rain, as the latter [and] former rain unto the earth.

• HE TOOK THE KEYS OF DEATH AND HELL (Rev 1:18)

He was dead and is alive evermore (Rev 1:18)

Jesus' death and resurrection was all in order to free us from the enemy of fear and death.

2 Tim 1:10 But is now made manifest by the appearing of our Saviour Jesus Christ, who hath abolished death,and hath brought life and immortality to light through the gospel:

The Message Bible paints this picture.

Rom 6:9 (Message) We know that when Jesus was raised from the dead it was a signal of the end of death-as-the-end. Never again will death have the last word.

Rom 6:10 (Message) When Jesus died, he took sin down with him, but alive he brings God down to us.

1 Thes 4:14 Since Jesus died and broke loose from the grave, God will most certainly bring back to life those who died in Jesus.

1 Thes 5:10 He died for us, a death that triggered life. Whether we're awake with the living or asleep with the dead, we're alive with him!

Rom 14:9 For Christ died and lived again for this very purpose, that He might be Lord both of the dead and of the living.

HE WAS THE FIRST BEGOTTEN FROM THE DEAD (REV 1:5)

If you die in Christ, the Bible calls it sleep and you will be raised again. The second death will have no hold on you.

1 Cor 15:20 But now is Christ risen from the dead, [and] become the first fruits of them that slept.

Death is the root cause of fear in the human race. Death reigned from Adam to Moses, when death was harnessed by the law, but the law could not bring life; it was a system of condemnation.

LIFE CAME THROUGH CHRIST.

Heb 2:14 Forasmuch then as the children are partakers of flesh and blood, he also himself likewise took part of the same; that through death he might destroy him that had the power of death, that is, the devil;

Heb 2:15 And deliver them who through fear of death were all their lifetime subject to bondage.

Rev 14:13 And I heard a voice from heaven saying unto me, Write, Blessed [are] the dead which die in the Lord from henceforth: Yea, saith the Spirit, that they may rest from their labours; and their works do follow them.

• HE LOVED US AND WASHED US FROM OUR SINS (REV 1:5)

We are the object of His love. We are the reason the bible exists. The whole book of Revelation has happened, on our behalf.

Col 1:14 In whom we have redemption through his blood, [even] the forgiveness of sins:

Col 2:14 Blotting out the handwriting of ordinances that was against us, which was contrary to us, and took it out of the way, nailing it to his cross;

• THE PRINCE OF THE KINGS OF THE EARTH (REV 1:5)

He made us kings and priests unto God and His Father (Rev 1:6)

Rev 19:16 And he hath on [his] vesture and on his thigh a name written, KING OF KINGS, AND LORD OF LORDS.

Rev 19:14 And the armies [which were] in heaven followed him upon white horses, clothed in fine linen, white and clean.

God's purposes are forever settled in the heavens. His Word cannot change. His Word was fulfilled about the Promised Land, yet it was a different generation that entered. The same happened from the old to the new.

Exo 19:6 And ye shall be unto me a kingdom of priests, and an holy nation. These [are] the words which thou shalt speak unto the children of Israel.

God's promises are established in Christ.

Matt 21:43 Therefore say I unto you, The kingdom of God shall be taken from you, and given to a nation bringing forth the fruits thereof.

Matt 21:45 And when the chief priests and Pharisees had heard his parables, they perceived that he spake of them.

Gods promises come to all who accept the sacrifice.

1 Pet 2:9 But you are a chosen race(generation), a royal priesthood, a dedicated nation, [God's] own purchased, special people, that you may set forth the wonderful deeds and display the virtues and perfections of Him Who called you out of darkness into His marvellous light.

• HE IS THE BEGINNING AND THE END (REV 1:8)

He is the Alpha and Omega (Rev 1:11)

God has no beginning or ending, he has no father or mother.

> **Heb 7:3** Without father, without mother, without descent, having neither beginning of days, nor end of life; but made like unto the Son of God; abideth a priest continually.

This has everything to do with what He is, for our sake.

> **Heb 12:2** Looking unto Jesus the author and finisher of [our] faith;

• HE IS SON OF MAN, SON OF GOD (REV 1:13)

Christ was the body prepared through the ages on whom the dove descended, and found a resting place, in order for salvation to come to humanity.

> **Gen 8:12** And he stayed yet other seven days; and sent forth the dove; which returned not again unto him anymore.

Jesus became that resting place.

> **John 1:32** And John bare record, saying, I saw the Spirit descending from heaven like a dove, and it abode upon him.
> 1:33 And I knew him not: but he that sent me to baptize with water, the same said unto me, Upon whom thou shalt see the Spirit descending, and remaining on him, the same is he which

baptizeth with the Holy Ghost.

1:34 And I saw, and bare record that this is the Son of God.

Mark 1:10 And straightway coming up out of the water, he saw the heavens opened, and the Spirit like a dove descending upon him:

1:11 And there came a voice from heaven, [saying], Thou art my beloved Son, in whom I am well pleased.

At His baptism, everything changed and He received the quickening Spirit: The Holy Spirit came down and dwelt in Him, the same time a voice from heaven declared Him to be the Christ, the Son of God. Immediately after that, He was led into the desert to be tempted by Satan, to deny this newly received Sonship.

AS SON OF MAN:
- Jesus preached that the Kingdom is at hand.
- Jesus broke bread with His disciples and said,

THIS IS MY BODY, and THIS IS MY BLOOD
- Jesus died and brought in the Kingdom. Their eyes opened when He broke bread again with them in the Kingdom.
- He ruled that generation for forty years with a

HE USED the ROD OF IRON until the Old was removed.
- He finished His work as the Son of Man. He removed the old and fully established the New.

• THE DOCTRINE OF CHRIST

2 John 1:9 Whosoever transgresseth, and abideth not in the doctrine of Christ, hath not God. He that abideth in the doctrine of Christ, he hath both the Father and the Son.

Jesus was not accepted as the Messiah, because they saw Him as a man, they knew his family and they knew where he grew up. He was continually confronted about who He really was, and He openly confessed that He was, The Christ, but the people expected something else.

Demons acknowledged Him to be the SON of God, but the religious leaders, just could not see it. Peter only recognized this truth by revelation, yet, the man that nailed Him to the Cross recognized Him as the Christ.

Mark 15:39 And when the centurion, who stood guard over Him, saw that as He cried out, and gave up the ghost, the centurion said," Truly, this Man was the Son of God."

Flesh and blood can only see these truths if the Spirit opens it up.

- HE WAS FROM ABOVE AND NOT FROM BENEATH.
-HE WAS IN THE WORLD, YET NOT FROM THE WORLD.

Jesus was born of God and fashioned in the form of man, then filled with all the fullness of God. He was the SON OF MAN, and at the same time He was the SON OF GOD

Heb 1:3 He is the sole expression of the glory of God [the Light-being, the out-raying or radiance of the divine], and He is the perfect imprint and very image of [God's] nature, upholding and maintaining and guiding and propelling the universe by His mighty Word of power.

It is not enough to receive Jesus; We have to embrace the Christ.

2 John 1:10 If there come any unto you, and bring not this doctrine, receive him not into [your] house, neither bid him God speed:

The revelation Peter got from the Father, that the "SON OF MAN is the SON OF GOD" is far more important than we have made it out to be. This is the place where God will build his church. The church is that place where man is dwelt by God; it is not a building, yet it is a building not made with hands. The church is not built on Peter or, the Christ; it is the combination of God and man.

A wise man that build his house on the rock. Now, God builds His church on those that are founded on the Rock. The church is not the building with bricks, it is His body, a house built with living stones. John calls this; "The doctrine of Christ".
This doctrine is inseparable from understanding and getting revelation in the Word and experiencing the life, light of God.

2 John 1:9 Whosoever transgresseth, and abideth not in the doctrine of Christ, hath not God. He that abideth in the doctrine of Christ, he hath both the Father and the Son.

We have to abide by God's purposes and plans.

> **1 John 3:8** …For this purpose, the Son of God was manifested, that he might destroy the works of the devil.
> - This is why Adam was created.
> - This is why Jesus came.
> - This is why you have received the Spirit; Creation is waiting for us to step into Sonship.

• THE COMING OF THE LORD (REV 1:7)

> **Rev 1:7** Behold, he cometh with clouds; and every eye shall see him, and they [also] which pierced him: and all kindreds of the earth shall wail because of him. Even so, Amen.

Confusion, has always been the result of misunderstanding God's purpose and plans, especially when it comes to His returning and end times. The coming of the Lord has always been a dispute amongst scholars. Many incorrect predictions have been made and are still being made, because of wrong interpretation of prophecy and ignorance about the difference in the purpose and workings of the "SON of MAN" and "SON of GOD".

The Son of Man came to deal with the sin question and to complete the work started on the cross. The book of Romans chapter eight confirms that He condemned sin in the flesh, as Son of Man.

Rom 8:3 For what the law could not do, in that it was weak through the flesh, God sending his own Son in the likeness of sinful flesh, and for sin, condemned sin in the flesh:

The Son of God, the victorious Lord of Glory, will return for His glorious church.

Heb 9:28 So Christ was once offered to bear the sins of many; and unto them that look for him shall he appear the second time without sin unto salvation.

• SON OF MAN COMING WITH THE CLOUDS

Rev 1:7 Behold, he cometh with clouds; and every eye shall see him, and they also which pierced him: and all kindreds of the earth shall wail because of him. Even so, Amen.

The clouds are not physical clouds that consists of water drops, but it is a spiritual cloud consisting of saints, God's people, who obtained a good report and have not yet received perfection. Hebrews twelve calls them the cloud of witnesses. They were souls in waiting for the new to break through.

This same coming is also described in the book of Daniel chapter seven, when the Son of Man entered, with the clouds of heaven where the Ancient of days was seated on the throne, as the judge in a courtroom situation. He took on our sin and was judged and condemned as the Son of Man.

> **Dan 7:13** I saw in the night visions, and, behold, [one] like the Son of Man came with the clouds of heaven, and came to the Ancient of days, and they brought him near before him.

Note; It is the Son of Man coming with the clouds of heaven and the people who would experience this coming, are the very ones that pierced Him. The Son of Man had to finish the work He came to do and that included the complete removing of the old and bringing in of the New.

Who pierced Him? That wicked generation of serpent seed that called for His blood to come on them and their children. A generation is forty years (4x10) and the forty years from the cross to the destruction of Jerusalem, marked that generation.

> **Matt 24:27** For as the lightning cometh out of the east, and shineth even unto the west; so shall also the coming of the Son of man be.
> **Matt 24:29** Immediately after the tribulation of those days shall the sun be darkened, and the moon shall not give her light, and the stars shall fall from heaven, and the powers of the heavens shall be shaken:

> **Rev 14:14** And I looked, and behold a white cloud, and upon the cloud [one] sat like unto the Son of man, having on his head a golden crown, and in his hand a sharp sickle.

The SON of MAN, came to finish the work started on the cross.

The Jews were scattered around the Mediterranean and did not even know what happened in Jerusalem. The gospel however, had to be preached to all of them first, before it could go to the other nations. He came to His own first, but they rejected and killed Him, and now they turned on His followers. Paul was thrown in prison, beaten and stoned.

> **Acts 13:46** Then Paul and Barnabas waxed bold, and said, It was necessary that the word of God should first have been spoken to you: but seeing ye put it from you, and judge yourselves unworthy of everlasting life, lo, we turn to the Gentiles.

JESUS died in Jerusalem in 30 AD. and the temple was burned down in 70 AD. The forty years that followed the Crucifixion and the end of that system of worship, was described in the book of Daniel chapter twelve, "and there shall be a time of trouble (Amp- tribulation), such as never was since there was a nation [even] to that same time:"

> **Rev 21:6** And he said unto me, It is done. I am Alpha and Omega, the beginning and the end. I will give unto him that is thirsty of the fountain of the water of life freely.

THE COMING OF THE SON OF MAN, is always coupled with Fear

> **Rev 6:14** And the heaven departed as a scroll when it is rolled together; and every mountain and island were moved out of their places.
> **Rev 6:15** And the kings of the earth, and the great men, and the rich men, and the chief captains, and the mighty men, and

every bondman, and every free man, hid themselves in the dens and in the rocks of the mountains;

Rev 6:16 And said to the mountains and rocks, Fall on us, and hide us from the face of him that sitteth on the throne, and from the wrath of the Lamb:

THE DAY OF THE LORD IS A THIEF IN THE NIGHT. GOD IS NOT A THIEF.

The very minute Judas ate the bread Satan entered him and when he left, the gross darkness started. IT WAS NIGHT.

Note; that 1 John was written after 70 AD.

1 John 2:8 Again, a new commandment I write unto you, which thing is true in him and in you: because the darkness is past, and the true light now shineth.

2 Pet 3:10 But the day of the Lord will come as a thief in the night; in the which the heavens shall pass away with a great noise, and the elements shall melt with fervent heat, the earth also and the works that are therein shall be burned up.

- SUDDEN DESTRUCTION

Matt 24:27 For as the lightning cometh out of the east, and shineth even unto the west; so shall also the coming of the Son of man be.
:30 And then shall appear the sign of the Son of man in heaven: and then shall all the tribes of the earth mourn, and they shall see the Son of man coming in the clouds of heaven with power

and great glory.

:31 And he shall send his angels with a great sound of a trumpet, and they shall gather together his elect from the four winds, from one end of heaven to the other.

The sounding of the trumpet here is working together with the four winds or forces of power on the earth and has to do with the removal of that old system. Clearly, this was not meant for the ones that accepted the sacrifice, for creation is waiting for the manifestation of the Sons of God.

2 Tim 1:7 For God hath not given us the spirit of fear; but of power, and of love, and of a sound mind.

The New Testament was written in anticipation and preparation for the Day of the Lord, which was clearly a 'day of Vengeance' and wrath.

The Word however, is Spirit breathed, and is always foreshadowing what is yet to come. What is, and what is to come, should not be mixed up, because it works out in different generations of people. You cannot be the wicked generation and the chosen generation at the same time.

The difference is very clearly seen in 1 Thessalonians.

1 Thes 5:1 But of the times and the seasons, brethren, ye have no need that I write unto you.

:2 For yourselves know perfectly that the day of the Lord so cometh as a thief in the night.

:3 For when they shall say, Peace and safety; then sudden

destruction cometh upon them, as travail upon a woman with child; and they shall not escape.

:4 But ye, brethren, are not in darkness, that that day should overtake you as a thief.

:5 Ye are all the children of light, and the children of the day: we are not of the night, nor of darkness.

:6 Therefore let us not sleep, as [do] others; but let us watch and be sober.

:7 For they that sleep sleep in the night; and they that be drunken are drunken in the night.

:8 But let us, who are of the day, be sober, putting on the breastplate of faith and love; and for an helmet, the hope of salvation.

:9 For God hath not appointed us to wrath, but to obtain salvation by our Lord Jesus Christ,

• THE COMING OF THE VICTORIOUS LORD

To those who accept Him, He will come again, as the victorious Lord of Glory. It will be announced with a trumpet, and we will be physically changed. This coming is not compared to a thief, but rather the returning of the saints.

1 Thes 1:10 And to wait for his Son from heaven, whom he raised from the dead, [even] Jesus, which delivered us from the wrath to come.

1 Thes 2:19 For what [is] our hope, or joy, or crown of rejoicing? [Are] not even ye in the presence of our Lord Jesus Christ at his coming?

1 Thes 3:13 To the end he may stablish your hearts unblameable in holiness before God, even our Father, at the coming of our Lord Jesus Christ with all his saints.

1 Thes 4:13 But I would not have you to be ignorant, brethren, concerning them which are asleep, that ye sorrow not, even as others which have no hope.

:14 For if we believe that Jesus died and rose again, even so them also which sleep in Jesus will God bring with him.

:15 For this we say unto you by the word of the Lord, that we which are alive [and] remain unto the coming of the Lord shall not prevent them which are asleep.

:16 For the Lord himself shall descend from heaven with a shout, with the voice of the archangel, and with the trump of God: and the dead in Christ shall rise first:

:17 Then we which are alive [and] remain shall be caught up together with them in the clouds, to meet the Lord in the air: and so shall we ever be with the Lord.

:18 Wherefore comfort one another with these words.

Compare what we have seen in the following scriptures.

Heb 9:28 So Christ was once offered to bear the sins of many; and unto them that look for him shall he appear the second time without sin unto salvation.

1 John 3:2 Beloved, now are we the sons of God, and it doth not yet appear what we shall be: but we know that, when he shall appear, we shall be like him; for we shall see him as he is.

1 Thes 4:16 For the Lord himself shall descend from heaven with a shout, with the voice of the archangel, and with the trump of God: and the dead in Christ shall rise first:

• HIS DOMINION FOREVER AND EVER (REV 1:18)

Satan for sure will not have the last say.

> **Dan 7:13** I saw in the night visions, and, behold, [one] like the Son of man came with the clouds of heaven, and came to the Ancient of days, and they brought him near before him.
> :14 And there was given him dominion, and glory, and a kingdom, that all people, nations, and languages, should serve him: his dominion [is] an everlasting dominion, which shall not pass away, and his kingdom [that] which shall not be destroyed.

• JESUS, THE LION, AND THE LAMB

In the book of Revelation chapter five, heaven was in an uproar because no-one could open the seals of the book, in the hands of the One on the throne. The Lion from the tribe of Judah was found worthy to break the seals, but then everything in heaven and earth took a turn as the Lamb took the book, and opened the seals. God had them in confusion according to Psalm two.
John the Baptist referred to the Lamb as the One slain to take away the sins of the world. Satan's so-called victory became his final defeat. The Lamb resembles the CRUCIFIED CHRIST.

Rev 5:5 And one of the elders saith unto me, Weep not: behold, the Lion of the tribe of Judah, the Root of David, hath prevailed to open the book, and to lose the seven seals thereof.

Rev 5:6 And I beheld, and, lo, in the midst of the throne and of the four beasts, and in the midst of the elders, stood a Lamb as it had been slain, having seven horns and seven eyes, which are the seven Spirits of God sent forth into all the earth.

Rev 5:7 And he came and took the book out of the right hand of Him that sat upon the throne.

The Lamb turned out to be the Lion.

Psa 2:4 He that sitteth in the heavens shall laugh: The Lord shall have them in derision.

HIS STRENGTH IS FOUND IN MEEKNESS

In Daniel six we find Daniel in a den surrounded by lions, but unable to harm him. This was a picture of what happened on the cross. Satan's so-called victory was his defeat.

In Revelation chapter fourteen, we see the Lamb, victorious, standing on Mount Zion, symbolizing the church with 144000, 1200 from every tribe, a perfect work.

• THE RIDER ON THE WHITE HORSE

Jesus came to destroy the works of the evil one, and to finish the work He started. He totally fulfilled the law and the prophets, and established the new, the Kingdom of God on earth.

> **Rom 8:3** For what the law could not do, in that it was weak through the flesh, God sending his own Son in the likeness of sinful flesh, and for sin, condemned sin in the flesh:

He is the ultimate Winner, the Rider on the white horse. He now calls us to ride with him and lay hold of what He has accomplished, the Crown of Eternal Life. No matter how Satan tries, it is finished and it is done. He can never change it. Nowhere is found a better description of the conquering Christ than in Revelation 19.

> **Rev 19:11** And I saw heaven opened, and behold a white horse, and he that sat upon him was called Faithful and True, and in righteousness he doth judge and make war.
> :12 His eyes were as a flame of fire, and on his head were many crowns; and he had a name written, that no man knew, but he himself.
> :13 And he was clothed with a vesture dipped in blood: and his name is called The Word of God.
> :14 And the armies which were in heaven followed him upon white horses, clothed in fine linen, white and clean.
> :15 And out of his mouth goeth a sharp sword, that with it he should smite the nations: and he shall rule them with a rod of iron: and he treadeth the winepress of the fierceness and wrath of Almighty God.
> :16 And he hath on his vesture and on his thigh a name written, KING OF KINGS, AND LORD OF LORDS.

A white horse resembles a conqueror. The first horse that ran when the seals were opened was a white horse and he came conquering, but brought in calamity. In Daniel two, King Nebuchadnezzar, is called; king of kings and lord of lord's, small letters.

> **Dan 2:37** Thou, O king, [art] a king of kings: for the God of heaven hath given thee a kingdom, power, and strength, and glory.

The spirit behind Babylon is to be equal with God. He tried to be a conqueror through earthly kingdoms and even allied with the Jews. He tried his best, but nothing on earth can match God.

> **Rev 21:6** And he said unto me, It is done. I am Alpha and Omega, the beginning and the end. I will give unto him that is athirst of the fountain of the water of life freely.

• JESUS CHRIST THE VICTORIOUS LORD

We cannot separate Jesus from the Message.

JESUS CHRIST DID NOT BRING THE ANSWER.
HE IS THE ANSWER.
HE IS THE TRUTH, THE WAY AND THE LIFE.
HE IS THE PLACE PREPARED FOR US

The Son of God became the Son of Man.
The Son of Man became the Christ through Spirit.
He laid down His life as the only begotten Son of God.

He became the final sacrificial Lamb, removing the sins of the world.

He paid the full price for all humanity.

He conquered as the Lion of Judah.

He became the Rider on the White Horse.

He broke the seals and unleashed the Day of Vengeance.

He finished the work He started and removed the old.

He will finally come as Lord of Glory, when we will be as He is.

Rom 8:31 What shall we then say to these things? If God [be] for us, who [can be] against us?

:32 He that spared not his own Son, but delivered him up for us all, how shall he not with him also freely give us all things?

:33 Who shall lay anything to the charge of God's elect? [It is] God that justifieth.

:34 Who [is] he that condemneth? [It is] Christ that died, yea rather, that is risen again, who is even at the right hand of God, who also maketh intercession for us.

:35 Who shall separate us from the love of Christ? [shall] tribulation, or distress, or persecution, or famine, or nakedness, or peril, or sword?

:36 As it is written, For thy sake we are killed all the day long; we are accounted as sheep for the slaughter.

:37 Nay, in all these things we are more than conquerors through him that loved us.

:38 For I am persuaded, that neither death, nor life, nor angels, nor principalities, nor powers, nor things present, nor things to come,

:39 Nor height, nor depth, nor any other creature, shall be able to separate us from the love of God, which is in Christ Jesus our Lord.

We do not have to add or adjust what Christ has done, and even though we are still in a fallen creation bound to time, not even death can pluck us from His hands.

GOD HAS NOT GIVEN US A SPIRIT OF FEAR.
WE JUST NEED A FRESH REVELATION OF JESUS.

The Church
CHAPTER TWO:

Mat 16:18
...I will build my church and the gates of Hell
shall not prevail against it.

We live in a time where Revelation is mostly used to prove some
fear driven, end-time doctrine and preaching is mostly from the
letters written by Paul, Peter, and John. All this is good, but it is not
complete, and we find churches without discernment, weak and
allowing things that God hates. The church has been pulled through
the mud because we have a wrong understanding of what and who
the church is.

The church is not a building or a denomination; it is Christ's body on
earth. That makes it THE most important place on earth, and we have
to get the right understanding of the purpose of God with and for His
Body, THE CHURCH.
God's purpose for the church is to be overcomers in this life. That
makes the understanding of the book of Revelation of utmost
importance.

• THE CHURCH IS A BODY

Earth is a very special place, and you need very special equipment to function on this beautiful, blue planet. God created us in an all-inclusive earth suite which is called a body.

Formed from the dust of the ground, the body is an amazing piece of work, that we so often take for granted. Our bodies are our most important possession on earth, because without it, we cannot function on this earth

Many people that had a near death experience, witnessed that they could see their bodies from the outside as well as, all the people around their bodies. Everything felt normal to them except, they could not function in their bodies.

Satan's problem is; he does not have a body, so that's why he uses alternative bodies to function on earth. He is an alien.
He first used a snake in the garden to deceive the woman and bring man down and lose the Glory of God. The war that already raged in heaven, was now brought to earth, and Satan deceived man away from God's purposes, causing enmity between the two seeds, good and evil. Satan then worked his plans through the bodies of this fallen humanity, planting his seed within them, trying to contaminate the Godly seed, but He that sits in the heavens laughs. Darkness can never overshadow light and God Himself was coming into this world to rescue man.

> **Heb 10:5** Wherefore when he cometh into the world, he saith, Sacrifice and offering thou wouldest not, but a body hast thou prepared me:

Rom 8:3 … God sending his own Son in the likeness of sinful flesh, and for sin, condemned sin in the flesh:

1 Pet 2:24 Who his own self bare our sins in his own body on the tree, that we, being dead to sins, should live unto righteousness: by whose stripes ye were healed.

Christ on earth, was God Manifested, the exact imprint of God.

Heb 1:3 He is the sole expression of the glory of God [the Light-being, the out-raying or radiance of the divine], and He is the perfect imprint and very image of [God's] nature,

1 Tim 3:16 And without controversy great is the mystery of godliness: God was manifest in the flesh, justified in the Spirit, seen of angels, preached unto the Gentiles, believed on in the world, received up into glory.

On the third day, after Christ died, Mary visited the grave. The stone was rolled away and where the body of Jesus was, just a few hours before, only garments were left. The head cloths were folded, but cloths from the body were just thrown down. Christ is the head of the church.

Where did He go?

He went to prepare us a place in the Spirit, His body on earth;

"THE CHURCH."

• THE CHURCH, IS A MYSTERY

His body was offered up to form a many, membered body, consisting of all that would believe in Him. The minute you are born again, you are sealed with the Spirit and forever connected to Him. You already have all you will ever need to live this new life, Christ being your head. This is a mystery; no flesh can work it out.

His intention is for all to grow up in His image and perfection, into the head. It is quite in order to have heroes of faith, BUT we are not to be become like them, we are to grow into Christ and be Christ on the earth. That is dying to self and taking on His character, no-one else's character will do.

The Greek word for church is; **ekklēsia, ;**
   a called out one, a religious congregation - assembly, church.

The Church, the "Ecclesia" is the Body of Christ on earth and we belong to each other and we fellowship with each other. Arguing about it does not make you part of the body, only living a connected life in the Spirit do.
We are all part of one big body and it does nobody good when we talk bad about the church. God is the head; He will take care of it. Separating yourself in a small groups and preaching about ecclesia does not make you part of the body. Christ is the head and it is HIS body.

The Epistles were written to the early church instructing the church on how to function and the Message Bible brings it out very clearly.

   Rom 12:3 I'm speaking to you out of deep gratitude for all that

God has given me, and especially as I have responsibilities in relation to you. Living then, as every one of you does, in pure grace, it's important that you not misinterpret yourselves as people who are bringing this goodness to God. No, God brings it all to you. The only accurate way to understand ourselves is by what God is and by what he does for us, not by what we are and what we do for him.

:4 In this way we are like the various parts of a human body. Each part gets its meaning from the body as a whole, not the other way around.

:5 The body we're talking about is Christ's body of chosen people. Each of us finds our meaning and function as a part of his body. But as a chopped-off finger or cut-off toe we wouldn't amount to much, would we? So since we find ourselves fashioned into all these excellently formed and marvelously functioning parts in Christ's body,

:6 let's just go ahead and be what we were made to be, without enviously or pride fully comparing ourselves with each other, or trying to be something we aren't. If you preach, just preach God's Message, nothing else;

:7 if you help, just help, don't take over; if you teach, stick to your teaching;

:8 if you give encouraging guidance, be careful that you don't get bossy; if you're put in charge, don't manipulate; if you're called to give aid to people in distress, keep your eyes open and be quick to respond; if you work with the disadvantaged, don't let yourself get irritated with them or depressed by them. Keep a smile on your face.

:9 Love from the center of who you are; don't fake it. Run for dear life from evil; hold on for dear life to good.

A functioning body is where members function in their calling.

You cannot cut yourself off from the body and then try and change doctrine that God has put in place. On the other hand sleeping in a garage does not make you a car; Going to church does not make you a Christian.

YOU HAVE TO BE BORN AGAIN.

Fifty days after the resurrection, they were endued with power from on high; receiving the same Spirit, that was in Christ and that is what binds His body together. The church is the object of all God's working on the earth, His body, His dwelling place.

The church is not a man made institution, but a Spirit birthed body. It cannot function by the flesh, yet it manifests in the flesh. That which is born of flesh, is flesh and that which is born of Spirit, is Spirit and the wind blows where it will.
Christ is the Head. We are the body. We are the temple. We are God's dwelling on the earth. We cannot go back and rebuild the shadow of a temple in the old Jerusalem.

> **1 Cor 6:19** What? Know ye not that your body is the temple of the Holy Ghost [which is] in you, which ye have of God, and ye are not your own?

We are now two thousand years later and we still in need of these instructions. The generation of Christ is a generation consisting of many generations, and the body consists of many members. Therefore God is patiently waiting for His body to grow into His full stature. He works where we do not even understand.

THE CHURCH IS NOT A BUILDING,
YET IT IS A SPIRITUAL HOUSE,
MADE WITH LIVING STONES,
THE BELIEVERS, WITH CHRIST AS THE HEAD.

• THE FUNCTIONING OF THE CHURCH

As our own bodies, so His body is well equipped for a life on earth, and it contains everything that it needs to survive. There are many systems in a body that functions and regulates itself automatically and without the effort of the brain instructing it. The heartbeat, hunger pains, goosebumps, sweat, these are all built in functions that work effortlessly to keep the body in line. If God has a body on this earth, you can be sure, that this body has everything built in, that it would need to be alive. Just wake up and do your part and stop trying to check others out.

Nowadays, there are so many cases of people that are not satisfied in themselves, with who they are and try to change their looks with plastic surgery and at the end totally distort their natural beauty. Some have even lost limbs and some their lives.

God is not the author of confusion and His body on earth has everything it needs to survive and overcome this world. There is place for everybody. There is place for every character and every talent and there is no reason to compete with anybody. WE are all equal important, we belong to each other. Every one gives the same amount, which is why our contribution is worked out in tithes.

There are enough finances, talents and callings in every church, in order for it to function properly. Finances is usually the biggest problem, and it is because the human mind develops a problem with math when, we get blessed financially. It is so easy to work out a tithe when we work with hundreds, but when we work with thousands we start adding our own thoughts to what we should contribute to the church. Well needless to say, when it comes to millions, we know exactly how to take the shortcuts.

The best is that we do not have to pay tithes, because we give everything. Well, then your tithe will be there between your, everything. Tithing is not because is not because of the law, it is because we are in Abraham's promise and part of His body. If mammon rules you, you might try or pretend, but you are not part of His body. Mammon cannot be your boss if you are Christ's body.

PLEASE, GET IT, A TITHE IS A TITHE.

Everybody contributes the same, despite the amount. In the spirit 100 can be the same as 1000000. Do not underestimate your part in the body. You are valuable to the body and to God.

The gifts are for the edifying of the body, they are not to uplift and enrich the individual. The gifts are to edify the body, not rip them off leaving it paralyzed and helpless, always having a shortage of money. For too long the church has been abused by so called; Men of God, who do not care for the body. Change is coming. All the workings of the Spirit from the book of Acts have been restored to the church, except Ananias and Sapphira, the dealing with mishandling of finances.

The body consists of believers, the seed of Abraham, who paid tithes 430 years before the law came into existence. Tithing works percentage wise and is totally impartial, for every member has the same responsibility. Teaching against tithing usually comes from teachers who do not take their responsibility in a local church or body, themselves. Satan is trying his best for the body not to function, but Christ is the head and the best is yet to come.

We need discernment in the church and we will get that, by reading the letters God wrote to the churches. Those letters are clear about what should be allowed and what should not be allowed in the Church, the body of Christ.

In a vision, John was on his way to the Holy of Holies, when he heard a voice behind him, and as he turned around, he saw one like the Son of man amongst the candlesticks. Immediately, God commanded John to write letters to the seven churches.

-The letters found in Revelation are directly from God, to bring the church to perfection. They are guidelines for the church, throughout all the ages, and it can only be lived out through the Spirit.

-The new Testament Epistles are the letters written by the apostles in the formation time of the church, during the mission journeys.

We have to know and understand God's heart for His church, to be overcomers in this world, not allowing the things that God actually hates, to destroy our faith. Chapter one, two and three of Revelation, describes the birth of the church.

> **Rev 1:20** The mystery of the seven stars which thou sawest in my right hand, and the seven golden candlesticks. The seven stars are the angels of the seven churches: and the seven candlesticks which thou sawest are the seven churches.

Seven is the number for the combination of heaven and earth, meaning God is working His plan on the earth.

Note: The stars are not on the candlesticks, but as soon as the door opened in heaven, we see the lamps on fire. (Rev 4:1) This signifies the birth of the church, Christ's body, on earth. Jesus is the door and he brought heaven to our realm, but you have to go through the door.

> **Rev 4:5** And out of the throne proceeded lightnings and thunderings and voices: and there were seven lamps of fire burning before the throne, which are the seven Spirits of God.

THE CHURCH WAS BORN

• THE PREPARATION of THE CHURCH

Israel was a body of people, a world prepared to bring salvation to all.

They carried the Ark of the Covenant with them for over 1500 years. Inside the ark was the testimonies of Christ, beneath the mercy seat where the presence of God appeared. In disobedience, they sinned themselves bankrupt, even though they carried the evidence of God's glory, they could not grasp God's plan. Israel broke every ordinance and command of God, but God stayed true to His promises and Christ the Messiah came as was promised.

> **Matt 15:24** But he answered and said, I am not sent, but unto the lost sheep of the house of Israel.

> **John 1:11** He came unto his own, and his own received him not.

> **John 19:15** But they cried out, "Away with Him, away with Him! Crucify Him!" Pilate said to them, "Shall I crucify your King?" The chief priests answered, "We have no king but Caesar!"

Even though the Jews in Jerusalem rejected Jesus, the gospel had to be preached to all Israel first, in order to fulfill the prophecies. Israel was His plan for salvation to the world. He came first to Israel, but He came for all.

• THE TRANSITION

After the death and the resurrection of Christ, Jesus commanded his disciples to preach the gospel to the whole world.

Jesus died in 30 AD., and forty years later, the temple was burned down in 70 AD. This was a very important and dramatic period. The temple in heaven was opened when Jesus died, yet no one could enter before the total removal of the old sacrificial system.

> **Heb 9:8** The Holy Ghost this signifying, that the way into the holiest of all was not yet made manifest, while as the first tabernacle was yet standing:

> **Rev 15:8** And the temple was filled with smoke from the glory of God, and from his power; and no man was able to enter into the temple, till the seven plagues of the seven angels were fulfilled.

The number forty represents a generation. Four meaning earthy and ten, complete. That was the time it took to remove the old and bring in the new, a whole generation. It also took forty years for Israel to enter into the Promised Land, a generation. We cannot change God's set times.

During the forty years from the Cross to the burning of Jerusalem:
- The Gospel had to reach the whole world.
- Persecution of Christians by the Jews started in Jerusalem.
- The Mission journeys of Paul took place.
- Churches sprang up around the Mediterranean.
- New Testament letters were written to all churches
- All the apostles died except John, the beloved.
- Rome's persecution increased
- The Jewish revolt started in 66 AD
- The Romans besieged Jerusalem 70AD.

- The destruction of Jerusalem and temple brought an end to the old system.

• THE INFANT CHURCH

The torn veil, proved the emptiness of the Holy of Holies. The Ark had disappeared during the captivity, but the Jews just kept on sacrificing. In doing that, they rejected the final sacrifice which Jesus had brought.

The gospel had to be preached to all the Jews first. At this point, many Jews were scattered around the Mediterranean Sea because of about five-hundred years of battles with the Babylonians, Medo-Persians, Greeks and Romans, as Daniel prophesied.

The Jewish people, scattered around the Mediterranean through all the wars, knew nothing of the crucifixion of Jesus and they were given another forty years to turn after Jesus died. It was their final chance at redemption, now on a personal level and not as a nation.

Paul was chosen by the Spirit, for this immense task. He was to reveal God's mysteries that were kept secret, to prepare His body on earth, the church, to rise. Paul was called to proclaim the gospel to the Gentiles, but he always preached in the synagogues first.
God did not institute Synagogues. It was part of their own system they birthed in Babylon. Time and again they threw Paul out of their synagogues, and he then preached to the Gentiles. For nearly thirty years, the gospel was preached to these people.

The mission journeys of Paul were known for the perils on the way, yet the cry in Paul's heart did not stop when he was jailed and beaten. The Spirit moved him ever onwards, and he wrote from prison;

Eph 1:16 Cease not to give thanks for you, making mention of you in my prayers;

:17 That the God of our Lord Jesus Christ, the Father of glory, may give unto you the spirit of wisdom and revelation in the knowledge of him:

:18 The eyes of your understanding being enlightened; that ye may know what is the hope of his calling, and what the riches of the glory of his inheritance in the saints,

:19 And what [is] the exceeding greatness of his power to us-ward who believe, according to the working of his mighty power,

:20 Which he wrought in Christ, when he raised him from the dead, and set [him] at his own right hand in the heavenly [places],

:21 Far above all principality, and power, and might, and dominion, and every name that is named, not only in this world, but also in that which is to come:

:22 And hath put all [things] under his feet, and gave him [to be] the head over all [things] to the church,

:23 Which is his body, the fullness of him that filleth all in all.

Mostly the Jews rejected the message and Paul was thrown out of their synagogues and imprisoned. Thus, they, brought the wrath of God on themselves, by rejecting God's ransom, bringing to fullness the sins of their fathers. However, the Gentiles began accepting the Word and churches sprang up all around the Mediterranean Sea, where the dispersed Jews settled.

The epistles, the New Testament letters, were written to these infant churches for guiding and encouragement and to teach them to hear with a spiritual ear, to understand the Kingdom. These were all written during the missionary journeys, and are part of the book of Acts.

Instead of accepting the opportunity that knocked on their door for the last time, the Jews rejected the Messiah and clung to the law, persecuting those who did receive the Christ.

> **Act 13:46** Then Paul and Barnabas waxed bold, and said, It was necessary that the word of God should first have been spoken to you: but seeing ye put it from you, and judge yourselves unworthy of everlasting life, lo, we turn to the Gentiles.

• THE INAUGURATION OF THE CHURCH

Thirty-six years after the crucifixion, John, the last remaining apostle, writes;

> **Rev 1:9** I John, who also am your brother, and companion in tribulation, and in the kingdom and patience of Jesus Christ, was in the isle that is called Patmos, for the word of God, and for the testimony of Jesus Christ.

John, caught up in the Spirit, on the day of the Lord and he turned around to see whose voice it was that spoke to him. There he found Christ amongst the candlesticks, He looked like Ancient of days and was holding the seven stars in His hands. It seems that all of the Word comes together at this point, the purpose of God is being revealed.

> **Rev 1:13** And in the midst of the seven candlesticks was one, like unto the Son of man,
> - He was clothed with a garment down to the foot, and girt about the paps with a golden girdle.
> - His head and his hairs were white like wool, as white as snow;
> - His eyes were as a flame of fire;
> - His feet like unto fine brass, as if they burned in a furnace;
> - His voice as the sound of many waters.

> **Dan 7:9** I beheld till the thrones were cast down, and the Ancient of days did sit,
> - Whose garment was white as snow,
> - The hair of his head like the pure wool:
> - His throne was like the fiery flame,
> - His wheels as burning fire.
> - A fiery stream issued and came forth from before him:
> Thousand, thousands ministered unto him, and ten thousand times ten thousand stood before him: the judgment was set, and the books were opened.

God now commanded John to write to the seven Churches.

God loves His creation and God loves His Church; clearly, He has been working through the ages and is now revealing his love for us through the Word, and will not forsake His creation. We are the objects of all His workings. We are to be His witnesses. He has given everything back into our hands and creation is now waiting for the revelation of the sons of God (Romans 8).

Revelation 1:5 He loved us, washed us and made us kings and priests to rule and reign on the earth and He is the prince of the Kings of the earth.

• THE LETTERS TO THE SEVEN CHURCHES

The time has arrived for the Kingdom of God to come in fullness, the birth of the church, including all nations, peoples, and tongues.

By this time, there were no more letters written to any church, for all the apostles, except one, had passed on to be with the Lord. John, the only apostle still alive, banned to a prison island in the Mediterranean, was commanded by God, Himself, to write seven letters to the seven churches in Asia.

> *THE LAST REMAINING APOSTLE WAS*
> *TO WRITE THE LAST LETTERS*
> *TO THE OVERCOMING CHURCHES,*
> *USHERING IN THE NEW ORDER OF WORSHIP*
> *IN THE SPIRIT.*

Never again would general letters be written to churches.

END IS A NEW BEGINNING.

Note: Jerusalem was not included, because God no longer acknowledged Jerusalem in the Middle East; the focus was now turned to the New Jerusalem, which is called; the Bride of the Lamb in the book of Revelation chapter twenty-one. This immediately connects the book of Genesis.

In chapter two of Genesis, God planted a garden Eastward in Eden, East meaning; "firstly", and garden meaning; "bride." God's plan has never changed.

The seven churches in Revelation represent all the churches, throughout all ages and time, to remind them to "Hear what the Spirit says." In all the letters to the churches, the call comes loud and clear, "If you have an ear to hear, HEAR what the SPIRIT says." It is the earnest heart of the Spirit pushing us forward to our heavenly calling.

The Spirit is not bound to one realm, it is multi-realm where time does not exist. These seven churches in Asia correlates with the Seven Church Ages through history. There are many interpretations to these periods, but it is clear that there are seven churches and seven church ages.

Here is an example of a breakup of the ages;

Ephesus	33-100 AD	Early Church
Smyrna	100-313 AD	Late Early Church
Pergamum	313-538 AD	Imperial Church
Thyatira	538-1514 AD	Dark Ages
Sardis	1514-1798 AD	Reformation Church
Philadelphia	1798-1866 AD	Missions Church
Laodicea	1866 AD	Modern Church

These messages from God, given by the Spirit, are of utmost

importance to all churches, throughout all the ages, not just in their certain time periods. There are no time periods in the Spirit. It does not matter where and when you live, what matters is; that you become an overcoming Christian.

It is time to study these letters, preach it in the churches and lead the people to be overcomers in this world.

• THE LETTERS TO THE SEVEN CHURCHES

1. GOD FIRST INTRODUCES HIMSELF TO EVERY CHURCH.

God walked with Adam in the garden, He spoke to Moses face to face as a friend, and He wants us to experience him. Man threw away that fellowship in disobedience, but God wants to dwell in us and He wants us to dwell in Him. God loves the world; therefore, He gave Himself to us. He constantly reveals himself to the church.

To;
- *Ephesus*-He who holds the seven **stars in His right hand,** who walks in the midst of the seven golden lampstands:
- *Smyrna*- The **First and the Last**, who was **dead, and came to life**.
- *Pergamum*-He who has the sharp **two-edged sword**:
- *Thyatira*- The Son of God, who has **eyes like a flame of fire**, and His feet like fine brass:
- *Sardis*-He who has the **seven Spirits of God and the seven stars**
- *Philadelphia*-He who is holy, He who is **true**, He who has the **key**

of David, He who opens and no one shuts, and shuts and no one opens.

- *Laodicea*-The Amen, **the Faithful and True Witness, the Beginning of the creation of God:**

2. SECONDLY, GOD ACKNOWLEDGE THEIR WORK.

- *Ephesus*- "I know your works, **your labour, your patience**, and that you cannot bear those who are evil and you have tested those who say they are **apostles and are not**, and have found them **liars**; and you have persevered and have patience, and **have laboured** for My name's sake and have not become weary."

- *Smyrna*-"I know your works, tribulation, and poverty (but you are rich); and I know the blasphemy of those who say they are **Jews** and are not, but are a **synagogue of Satan**."

- *Pergamum*-"I know your works, where you dwell, where Satan's throne is. And you hold fast to My name, and did not deny My faith even in the days in which Antipas was My faithful martyr, who was killed among you, where Satan dwells."

- *Thyatira*- "I know your works, love, service, faith, and your patience; and as for your works, the last are more than the first."

- *Sardis*-:"I know your works. Thou hast a few names even in Sardis which have not defiled their garments; and they shall walk with me in white: for they are worthy.

- *Philadelphia*- "I know your works for you have a little strength, have **kept My word**, and have not denied My name."
- *Laodicea*-"I know your works, that you are neither **cold nor hot.**"

3. THIRDLY, GOD REPRIMANDS THE CHURCHES.

- *Ephesus*- Nevertheless I have this against you, that you have **left your first love.**
- Pergamum- But I have a few things against you, because you have there those who hold the **doctrine of Balaam**, who taught Balak to put a stumbling-block before the children of Israel,to eat things sacrificed to idols, to commit sexual immorality. Thus you also have those who hold the **doctrine of the Nicolaitans**, which thing I hate."
- *Thyatira*- "I have a few things against you, because you allow that woman **Jezebel**, who calls herself a prophetess, to teach and seduce My servants to commit **sexual immorality and eat things sacrificed to idols.** And I gave her time to repent of her sexual immorality, and she did not repent. Indeed, I will cast her into a sickbed, and those who commit adultery with her into great tribulation, unless they repent of their deeds. I will kill her children with death, and all the churches shall know that I am He who searches the minds and hearts. And I will give to each one of you according to your works.
- *Sardis*- If therefore thou shalt not watch, I will come on thee as a thief, and thou shalt not know what hour I will come upon thee.

- **Laodicea**- "I could wish you were **cold or hot**. So then, because you are lukewarm, and neither cold nor hot, I will vomit you out of My mouth. Because you say, "I am rich, have become wealthy, and have need of nothing'-and do not know that you are wretched, miserable, poor, blind, and naked"

NOTE: God was satisfied with only two churches: Smyrna and Philadelphia.

4. GOD INSTRUCTS EVERY CHURCH.

- **Ephesus**- "Remember therefore from where you have fallen; repent and do the first works. Be watchful, and strengthen the things which remain, that are ready to die, do the **first works**, or else I will come to you quickly and remove your lampstand from its place-unless you repent."
- **Smyrna** – "Do not fear any of those things which you are about to suffer. Indeed, the devil is about to throw some of you into prison, that you may be tested, and you will have tribulation ten days."
- **Pergamum**- "Repent, or else I will come to you quickly and will fight against them with the sword of My mouth."
- **Thyatira**-"Now to you I say, and to the rest in Thyatira, as many as do not have this doctrine, who have not known the depths of Satan, as they say, I will put on you no other burden. But hold fast what you have till I come."
- **Sardis** – "Be watchful, and strengthen the things which remain, that are ready to die,remember therefore how you have

received and heard; hold fast and repent.

- *Philadelphia*- "Behold, I am coming quickly! Hold fast what you have, that no one may take your crown."
- *Laodicea*- "I counsel you to buy from Me gold refined in the fire, that you may be rich; and white garments, that you may be clothed, that the shame of your nakedness may not be revealed; and anoint your eyes with eye-salve, that you may see. As many as I love, I rebuke and chasten. Therefore, be zealous and repent. Behold, I stand at the door and knock. If anyone hears My voice and opens the door, I will come into him and dine with him, and he with Me."

5. GOD REWARDS FOR EVERY CHURCH.

- *Ephesus*- "To him who overcomes I will give to **eat from the tree of life,** which is in the midst of the Paradise of God."
- *Smyrna*- "Be faithful until death, and I will give you the **crown of life.**
- *Pergamum*- "To him who overcomes I will give of the hidden manna to eat. And I will give him a **white stone**, and on the stone **a new name** written which no one knows except him who receives it."
- *Thyatira* – "He who overcomes, and keeps My works until the end, to him I will give power over the nations- He shall rule them with **a rod of iron**; They shall be dashed to pieces like the potter's vessels' - as I also have received from My Father; and I will give him the morning star."

- *Sardis* –He who overcomes shall be clothed in **white garments**, and I will not blot out his name from the **Book of Life;** but I will confess his name before My Father and before His angels."
- *Philadelphia*- "See, I have set before you an open door, no one can shut it. Indeed, I will make those of the **synagogue of Satan**, who say they are Jews and are not, but lie-in deed I will make them come and worship before your feet, and to know that I have loved you. Because you have kept My command to persevere, I also will keep you from the **hour of trial which shall come upon the whole world,** to test those who dwell on the earth. He who overcomes, I will make him a pillar in the temple of My God, and he shall go out no more. I will write on him the name of My God and the name of the city of My God, the **New Jerusalem**, which comes down out of heaven from My God. And I will write on him **My new name.**"
- *Laodicea* – "To him who overcomes I will grant to **sit with Me on My throne**, as I also overcame and sat down with My Father on His throne."

THE REWARD FOR EVERY OVERCOMER, IS SONSHIP.

He wants us to make it so much, that He became our forerunner and went right into the veil, which is the anchor for our souls. We do not fight to win, the battle is won, we just have to lay hold of what he has accomplished, His Spirit helping us along.

NOTE: All the rewards have to do with the new Jerusalem lifestyle.

• THE THINGS GOD DOES NOT WANT IN HIS CHURCH

There are people found amongst believers that are not accepted by God, and they are not part of the church, the body of Christ. It does not matter what your personal opinion on these matters is, God does not want them to be allowed amongst His people. They are clearly identified throughout these letters.

- Those who say they are apostles, and are not.
- That woman Jezebel, being a false prophet.
- Those who hold the doctrine of the Nicolaitans, abusing God's
        grace,lording over God's people
- Those who hold the doctrine of Balaam, laying stumbling blocks for
        God's people for money.
-Those who say they are Jews and are not, but are a synagogue of
        Satan.

These are stumbling blocks to churches and should not be allowed.

Do not consider their personality or any natural appearance, discern the evil spirit working in them and do not allow them to work in the church, thus spreading serpent seed.

• HEAR WHAT THE SPIRIT SAYS

People are running around chasing every new wave in the church. It is not all together wrong, but why should we be bound only to the waves if there is an ocean to explore and enjoy. The Word does not state that we must hear what the preacher says, we have to hear what the Spirit says, then we will not be lead astray.

We cannot go back to the law, because we have to now hear what the Rabbi is saying. Whoever is preaching, they are not the Spirit and are not perfected yet. That does not mean we do not have to listen to anyone, NO, we have to learn to hear the voice of the Spirit.

> **1 Cor 1:21** For after that in the wisdom of God the world by wisdom knew not God, it pleased God by the foolishness of preaching to save them that believe.

> **1 John 2:27** But the anointing which ye have received of him abideth in you, and ye need not that any man teach you: but as the same anointing teacheth you of all things, and is truth, and is no lie, and even as it hath taught you, ye shall abide in him.

God has not purposed for the church to be blind, naked and self-enriched. He is coming for an overcoming church, and He, Himself made it possible, we just have to follow.

> **Rom 12:1** So here's what I want you to do, God helping you: Take your everyday, ordinary life-your sleeping, eating, going-to-work, and walking-around life-and place it before God as an offering. Embracing what God does for you is the best thing you can do for him.

Rom 12:3 The only accurate way to understand ourselves is by what God is and by what he does for us, not by what we are and what we do for him.

To every church, God writes;

"HE THAT HAS AN EAR TO HEAR, HEAR WHAT THE SPIRIT SAYS".

This is the only way you can live your Christian life.

These letters form God's plan for the church, His body on earth. They contain instructions for the "do's and the don'ts", they reprimand, warn, encourage, guide and instruct us on behaviour in the church. It has clear doctrinal guidelines with promised rewards that await every overcomer.

They cannot be ignored and should be read by the individuals as well as whole assemblies, throughout all the church ages, in order to "Hear what the Spirit says".

Eph 1:22 HE hath put all things under his feet, and gave him to be the head over all things to the church,
:23 Which is his body, the fullness of him that filleth all in all.

• THE REVEALING OF GOD'S FACE

Moses was not allowed to see the face of God, yet he was speaking to God face to face. He could only see the beginning of creation and

God's plan and it brought a change to his countenance.

Moses could not behold the face of God because of the Glory. Coming down the mountain the people could not behold the face of Moses, because of the glory of the past. He had to put a vail over his face, because of his face shining from the glory that was fading.

> **2 Cor 3:7** But if the ministration of death, written [and] engraven in stones, was glorious, so that the children of Israel could not stedfastly behold the face of Moses for the glory of his countenance; which [glory] was to be done away:
> :8 How shall not the ministration of the spirit be rather glorious?
> :9 For if the ministration of condemnation [be] glory, much more doth the ministration of righteousness exceed in glory.
> :11 For if that which is done away [was] glorious, much more that which remaineth [is] glorious.

The Spirit is that place of freedom, where the Glory of God is fully revealed. Revelation is a way of life.

> **2 Cor 3:16** Nevertheless when it shall turn to the Lord, the vail shall be taken away.
> :17 Now the Lord is that Spirit: and where the Spirit of the Lord [is], there [is] liberty.
> :18 But we all, with open face beholding as in a glass the glory of the Lord, are changed into the same image from glory to glory, [even] as by the Spirit of the Lord.

Jesus Christ is the face of God, the plan of God, the Glory of God revealed. He was the Word in the beginning and The Word is the rider on the white horse at the end. He is our rock and the place prepared by the Father.

2 Cor 4:6 For God, who commanded the light to shine out of darkness, hath shined in our hearts, to [give] the light of the knowledge of the glory of God in the face of Jesus Christ.

The manifested Christ was God's plan of bringing His Kingdom to earth.

Heb 1:3

He is the sole expression of the glory of God
[the Light-being, the out-raying or radiance of the divine], and He
is the perfect imprint and very image of [God's] nature,
upholding and maintaining and guiding
and propelling the universe by His mighty word of power.
When He had by offering Himself accomplished our cleansing
of sins and riddance of guilt,
He sat down
at the right hand of the divine Majesty on high,

THE ADVERSARY
CHAPTER THREE:

1Pe 5:8
Be sober, be vigilant;
because your adversary the devil, as a roaring lion,
walketh about, seeking whom he may devour:

In Genesis, we find Satan in the form of a serpent. He grew in
stature and became more subtle. His lies became more intense, and
in Revelation twelve, he is called; that old serpent, the "Great Red
Dragon."

• THE BATTLE OF THE AGES

God formed a body from dust, blew His breath into it and Adam
became a living soul within a body. To have a body is the only way
that anyone can operate on the earth. Adam was to rule and have
dominion over all God's creation. However, when he opened his eyes
in paradise, Satan was already there, waiting to deceive him.

From the start, it is clear that this fallen being, from the previous age,
is now challenging God's authority on earth, but he lacked a body.
Satan had to use the body of an animal, the snake, to do his dirty
work of deception, which originates from a spirit of rebellion.
As usual, one thing lead to another and everybody wants to blame
someone else. Instead of ruling, Adam listened to his wife and then

blamed her, who in turn listened to Satan. In their disobedience to God, they lost the light life and it ignited the battle of the ages between the two seeds; good and evil.

ENMITY WAS SET BETWEEN SATAN'S SEED, AND THE WOMAN'S SEED.

• TWO SEEDS, TWO BODIES

Gen 3:15 And I will put enmity between thee and the woman, and between thy seed and her seed; it shall bruise thy head, and thou shalt bruise his heel.

Now, we all know a woman does not carry seed, and we know that Mary knew no man, but she was overshadowed by the Spirit. God himself took on this war on behalf of all creation.

Right from the word go, Satan worked hard at infiltrating and perverting the seed line of God. Over and over he tried to kill and destroy the seed or damage the seed line. He entered the first human seed and Cain opened the door to sin and killed his brother, but:
Gen 4:25 … Adam knew his wife again; and she bare a son, and called his name Seth: For God, hath appointed me another seed instead of Abel, whom Cain slew.
Satan then tried to infiltrate the seed line of the sons of God, in Seth. The sons of God from the seed line of Seth, married the daughters of man, from the seed line of Cain, daughters of man, and sin spread like wildfire and giants were produced.

Please note: Angels were never called sons.

Heb 1:5 For unto which of the angels said he at any time, Thou art my Son, this day have I begotten thee? And again, I will be to him a Father, and he shall be to me a Son?

Sin became so rampant and the whole world became evil, only Noah was found righteous in his generation. At that point God regretted making man, and the first world was totally destroyed by water.

No one ever became older than a thousand years within the first spiritual day; in spite the fact that man was not suppose to die at all. Man was actually created to live forever, but now they all died within a thousand years. Not only did they die, the first world was totally destroyed.

Peter reminded us that; one day is as a thousand years, for God.

2 Pe 3:8 But, beloved, be not ignorant of this one thing, that one day is with the Lord as a thousand years, and a thousand years as one day.

The end spells a new beginning with God. There was a new beginning with Noah and all who came through the ark. Unfortunately, sin entered man in and now it came through the flood and just like rodents that come on ships destroy the nature of a beautiful island, sin manifested right after the flood and filled the earth once more.

Men became so arrogant, to a point that they now attempted to be God and built a city that would reach heaven. Once again God intervened and stopped man from destroying himself. God confused their languages and men scattered over the world in different directions, all building their own little kingdoms.

God loves his creation and called a man and revealed His redemption plan to him. Abraham, passed the test, and believed God. He moved away from everything that seemed right in the natural, and he left the earthly kingdom where he lived and went looking for a city that had foundations, whose builder and maker is God, on God's command.

The covenant with Abraham was established in two seed lines.

1. IN THE GENERATIONS.
2.IN THE PROMISE OF ONE SEED; IN CHRIST.

Gen 17:7 And I will establish my covenant between me and thee and thy seed after thee in their generations for an everlasting covenant, to be a God unto thee, and to thy seed after thee

The seed line covenant unfolded four hundred and thirty-years later, through Moses, through the seed in their natural generations. Satan went to the uttermost in destroying the seed line of redemption, but he could not touch the spiritual seed.

He worked through Pharaoh who massacred, a whole generation of baby boys. Ironically, Moses the target and reason for this massacre grew up, and was schooled by Pharaoh himself. This is proof that he is not as clever as people want us to believe. It is actually pathetic, and it was foreshadowing what was to happen with the baby Jesus and then the church.

The chosen people broke every command of life before Moses was able to impart God's plan to them. Satan then totally infiltrated the pattern that God gave Moses, and they became; "serpent seed".

The generational seed of Abraham were now totally corrupted and God himself came to redeem mankind, through the promised seed. We are not from a generational seed line that failed, but we are directly under the promise that was given Abraham and all we have to do is: BELIEVE. It was a built in guarantee from the beginning in order to secure the seed.

Satan used the wicked king Herod to try and get rid of the Christ, and once again he just could not get the right baby. Satan is NO match for God, and never will be. He could not stop God's plan.

> **Gal 4:4** But when the fullness of the time was come, God sent
>   forth his Son, made of a woman, made under the law,
> :5 To redeem them that were under the law, that we might receive
>   the adoption of sons.

God now had to redeem, not only the gentiles, but also them that were stuck in the system taken over by Satan himself. God himself stepped in to redeem creation. Satan's plans did not work and will never work. Now he is defeated, disarmed and his head is smashed. He is not to bright and God is not going to let him have the last say.

Gal 3:16 Now to Abraham and his seed were the promises made. He saith not, and to seeds, as of many; but as of one, and to thy seed, which is Christ.

• THE THREE FROG SPIRITS

Satan cannot create and there is nothing original in him; he can only copy. He got himself two friends and formed his own satanic trinity:

Rev 16:13 And I saw three unclean spirits like frogs [come] out of the mouth of
1. the dragon, and out of the mouth of
2. the beast, and out of the mouth of
3. the false prophet.

The Jews became the false prophet, who also formed an alliance with Rome, who resembled the beast and is symbolized by iron, Together they worked up their own army against the Messiah. All this was empowered by Satan, the dragon. They were doomed from the start, as they are no match for God.

Psa 2:1 Why do the heathen rage, and the people imagine a vain thing?
:2 The kings of the earth set themselves, and the rulers take counsel together, against the LORD, and against his anointed, [saying],
:3 Let us break their bands asunder, and cast away their cords from us.
:4 He that sitteth in the heavens shall laugh: the Lord shall have them in derision.

They all had one mind and one purpose.

> **Rev 17:13** These have one mind, and shall give their power and
> strength unto the beast.
> :14 These shall make war with the Lamb, and the Lamb shall
> overcome them: for he is Lord of lords, and King of kings: and
> they that are with him [are] called, and chosen, and faithful.

The only reason why the Dragon, the Beast and the False Prophet are mentioned in the book of Revelation is because they were defeated by the Lamb at Armageddon, the cross. They are definitely not symbols to scare Christians with.

ARMAGEDDON MEANS;
A HIGH PLACE WHERE STRENGTH IS MEASURED.

Jesus came as a Lamb to the slaughter, but when He gave up the ghost (spirit), then the Lion roared, and Satan was stripped of his power. The only thing he can do now is to deceive people, but his destiny is now set for sure.

> **Rev 20:10** And the devil that deceived them was cast into the lake
> of fire and brimstone, where the beast and the false prophet
> [are], and shall be tormented day and night forever and ever.

1. THE BEAST

There are so many explanations about the Beast doing the rounds, but Scripture must explain Scripture. It cannot be a king, and the next minute it is some big computer. We have to go back to the book of Daniel in order to explain the Beast.

In the book of Daniel chapter two, Nebuchadnezzar had a dream of a statue that consisted of gold, silver, bronze and iron and it resembled four empires that followed in succession, coming from the people, the kingdoms of the earth. The number four means earthly.
These empires were:

- GOLD - Babylon –   King Nebuchadnezzar
- SILVER - Medo-Persia -   King Cyrus
- BRONZE - Greece -   Alexander the Great
- IRON - Rome -   The Julio-Claudian Dynasty

A rock was cut lose without man's hands and struck this statue on the feet of iron and clay, and then became a high mountain that filled all the earth. That mountain is none other than Christ, the rock the builders rejected.

A body is controlled by the head and the three empires that followed; all got their inspiration from Babylon, which in turn was controlled by the same spirit that was working behind the tower of Babel. Satan was establishing his seed, in preparation for the final battle.

In chapter three, Nebuchadnezzar revealed the spirit that was working behind this statue when he made an entire statue of gold and made people bow before it. This statue resembled the image of the beast, which are the systems that control the worldly empires- the spirit of ANTI CHRIST. It is still working in the world.

In chapter seven, Daniel dreamed about four beasts that came out of the sea in succession. They represented the same empires as was revealed by the statue in King's Nebuchadnezzar's dream:

- Gold - [the Babylonian empire under Nebuchadnezzar] was like a lion and had eagle's wings.
- Silver - [the Medo-Persian empire] was like a bear. It raised up itself on one side [or one dominion] and three ribs were in its mouth between its teeth.
- Bronze - [the Grecian empire of Alexander the Great] like a leopard which had four wings of a bird on its back and four heads.
- Iron-[the Roman empire] terrible, powerful and dreadful, and exceedingly strong. It had great iron teeth; it devoured, crushed and trampled what was left with its feet. It was different from all the beasts that came before it, and it had ten horns [symbolizing ten kings].

These dreams run parallel but is progressive in revelation and cannot be interpreted by only reading one portion of the Word. We find this same story in the book of Revelation thirteen, the only difference being the four beasts are combined as one beast. In Daniel two four kingdoms form one body, and Babylon is the head. They all have the same purpose.

> **Rev 13:1** And I stood upon the sand of the sea, and saw a beast rise up out of the sea, having seven heads and ten horns, and upon his horns ten crowns, and upon his heads the name of

blasphemy.

:2 And the beast which I saw was like unto a leopard, and his feet
were as [the feet] of a bear, and his mouth as the mouth of
a lion: and the dragon gave him his power, and his seat, and
great authority.

The four empires operated through the same spirit and were
empowered by the dragon. The emblem of Babylon was a lion and in
the book of Revelation thirteen, the beast's mouth was like a lion.

Note: The dragon and the beast each had ten horns, and the Dragon
had seven heads; they all operated under and through the authority
and rulers. They are of the same kind and the same spirit, with one
mind; "To take out the Christ"., Psalm two.

-THE TEN HORNS

The last empire that Daniel saw in chapter seven, was Rome. It had
ten horns representing ten kings, of which three kings gave way to
one, that had a mouth speaking great things.

Dan 7:7 After this I saw in the night visions, and behold, a fourth
beast [the Roman empire]-terrible, powerful and dreadful, and
exceedingly strong. And it had great iron teeth; it devoured
and crushed and trampled what was left with its feet. And it
was different from all the beasts that came before it, and it had
ten horns [symbolizing ten kings].

:8 I considered the horns, and behold, there came up among them
another horn, a little one, before which three of the first horns
were plucked up by the roots; and behold, in this horn were

eyes like the eyes of a man and a mouth speaking great things. The first Roman Emperors in the Julio-Claudian dynasty:

1. Julius Caesar   - 27 BC
2. Augustus Caesar   - 27 BC - 14 AD
3. Tiberius Caesar   - 14 AD – 37 AD
4. Caligula Caesar   - 37 AD - 41 AD
5. Claudius Caesar   - 41 AD – 54 AD
6. Nero Caesar   - 54 AD – 68 AD

The next three were Caesars in one year.

7. Galba Caesar   - 68 AD -69 AD
8. Otto Caesar   - 69 AD
9. Vitellius Caesar   -69 AD
10. Vespasian Caesar   - 69 AD - 79 AD

THE SAME TEN HORNS
ARE DESCRIBED IN CONNECTION WITH THE BEAST
IN REVELATION THIRTEEN AND SEVENTEEN.

Flavian Dynasty was started when Vespasian received a prophecy that He would be Caesar. He turned from taking over Judea and went back to Rome and being a man of war, he easily conquered the throne.

> **Rev 17:12** And the ten horns which thou sawest are ten kings, which have received no kingdom as yet; but receive power as kings one hour with the beast.
> :13 These have one mind, and shall give their power and strength unto the beast.
> :14 These shall make war with the Lamb, and the Lamb shall

overcome them: for he is Lord of lords, and King of kings: and they that are with him [are] called, and chosen, and faithful.

:15 And he saith unto me, The waters which thou sawest, where the whore sitteth, are peoples, and multitudes, and nations, and tongues.

:16 And the ten horns which thou sawest upon the beast, these shall hate the whore, and shall make her desolate and naked, and shall eat her flesh, and burn her with fire.

:17 For God hath put in their hearts to fulfil his will, and to agree, and give their kingdom unto the beast, until the Words of God shall be fulfilled.

The ten horns now turned on the whore that was riding the Beast and destroyed her with fire. Rome destroyed the city and the temple, the seat of the false prophet, the whore.

2. THE FALSE PROPHET – THE HARLOT

Moses was given the instructions and foreshadowing pattern of the heavenly realm which was to be opened on the earth. A nation was prepared as a body, a system, to harness sin and death. The law system was only showing the way to Christ, who would redeem the sin of the world.

As a chosen nation, Israel carried the Testimonies of Christ with them, in the Ark, wherever they went for over one thousand-five-hundred years. Christ was with them all the time. They were the custodians of salvation.

1 Cor 10:3 They all eat the same spiritual meat

:4 And did all drink the same spiritual drink: for they drank of that spiritual Rock that followed them: and that Rock was Christ.

This nation was symbolised by a woman that was to bring forth the Man Child, the Saviour.

Gal 4:4 But when the fullness of the time was come, God sent forth his Son, made of a woman, made under the law,

Mary was a woman and the law was a woman.

Rev 12:1 And there appeared a great wonder in heaven; a woman clothed with the sun, and the moon under her feet, and upon her head a crown of twelve stars:

Joseph had a dream about the sun, moon and stars, a picture of the Israel, God's chosen people. The sun and the moon and the stars came and bowed before the one with the multi-colour coat, a picture of Jesus fulfilling all the law and the prophets. Salvation to all nations was God's plan from the beginning.

This system, the heavenly elements, was totally infiltrated by Satan, to the point that the Jews returning from Babylon worshipped the system and took it in their own control. Instead of receiving their Messiah they crucified Him and called for His blood to come on them. They became the fig tree within the Vine.

Matt 23:2 Saying, The scribes and the Pharisees sit in Moses' seat:

Unwilling to change, this chosen nation adulterated themselves bankrupt with the idols of nations around them. They killed the prophets that God sent to warn them, until they became captives in the very land that symbolises the spirit of the Anti-Christ: The head of the image of the Beast; Babylon. This marks the starting point of the destruction of Jerusalem and its temple.

> **Isa 43:14** Thus saith the LORD, your redeemer, the Holy One of Israel; For your sake I have sent to Babylon...

In Babylon, instead of repenting, they took their rebellion to a higher level. There they created their own system of worship and instituted Pharisees, Sadducees and Synagogues, which all became an abomination in God's eyes. Jesus called them "Serpent Seed" and "Vipers." He knew what their angle was.

The Ark disappeared when they were taken to Babylon. On returning from exile, they rebuilt their temple, without the Ark in the Holy of Holies. The Ark that represented God's presence, disappeared and now they just kept empty rituals, without God.
They killed God's prophets and now they allied with Rome to kill God's Son. No wonder Isaiah cries out:

> **Isa 1:21** How is the faithful city become a harlot! it was full of judgment; righteousness lodged in it; but now murderers.

The book of Revelation, chapter seventeen, describes this harlot riding on the scarlet coloured beast having seven heads and ten horns. She was full of the names of blasphemy and on her forehead was written: BABYLON THE GREAT, mother of harlots.

She became what she worshipped.

> **Rev 17:1** And there came one of the seven angels which had the
> seven vials, and talked with me, saying unto me, Come hither;
> I will shew unto thee the judgment of the great whore that
> sitteth upon many waters.
> :2 With whom the kings of the earth have committed fornication,
> and the inhabitants of the earth have been made drunk with
> the wine of her fornication.
> :3 So he carried me away in the spirit into the wilderness: and I
> saw a woman sit upon a scarlet coloured beast, full of names of
> blasphemy, having seven heads and ten horns.
> :4 And the woman was arrayed in purple and scarlet colour, and
> decked with gold and precious stones and pearls, having a
> golden cup in her hand full of abominations and filthiness of
> her fornication:
> 5 And upon her forehead [was] a name written, MYSTERY,
> BABYLON THE GREAT, THE MOTHER OF HARLOTS
> AND ABOMINATIONS OF THE EARTH.
> :6 And I saw the woman drunken with the blood of the saints, and
> with the blood of the martyrs of Jesus: and when I saw her, I
> wondered with great admiration.

The very woman (nation) that was to bring forth the Christ, turned
to harlotry and was made drunk with the blood of the Prophets and
rode the beast.

> **Rev 17:18** And the woman which thou sawest is that great city,
> which reigneth over the kings of the earth.

The very system that was to bring forth the Christ now became the false prophet, turning against the Christ, riding the Beast. The Jews allied with Rome to do their dirty work, but Satan could not stop God's Seed filling the earth. Not even by infiltrating the very woman that was to bring forth the Man Child. God had them in derision. They were no match for God and their ultimate fate is the lake of fire.

> **Rev 20:10** And the devil that deceived them was cast into the lake of fire and brimstone, where the beast and the false prophet [are], and shall be tormented day and night forever and ever.

-THE SEVEN HEADS

The rulers of the temple made an alliance with the rulers of the world in order to accomplish their wicked plans. All this was prophesied, and yet they blindly stumbled ahead to their own destruction.

David's prophesy a thousand years before describes this battle, the alliances made, as well as the outcome.

> **Psa 2:1** Why do the heathen rage, and the people imagine a vain thing?
> :2 The kings of the earth set themselves, and the rulers take counsel together, against the LORD, and against his anointed, [saying],
> :3 Let us break their bands asunder, and cast away their cords from us.
> :4 He that sitteth in the heavens shall laugh: the Lord shall have them in derision.
> :5 Then shall he speak unto them in his wrath, and vex them in his sore displeasure.

:6 Yet have I set my king upon my holy hill of Zion.

:7 I will declare the decree: the LORD hath said unto me, Thou [art] my Son; this day have I begotten thee.

:8 Ask of me, and I shall give [thee] the heathen [for] thine inheritance, and the uttermost parts of the earth [for] thy possession.

:9 Thou shalt break them with a rod of iron; thou shalt dash them in pieces like a potter's vessel.

:10 Be wise now therefore, O ye kings: be instructed, ye judges of the earth.

:11 Serve the LORD with fear, and rejoice with trembling.

:12 Kiss the Son, lest he be angry, and ye perish [from] the way, when his wrath is kindled but a little. Blessed [are] all they that put their trust in him.

Peter clearly revealed the rulers of Psalm two, when he explained to them the healing of the lame man.

Acts 3:12 And when Peter saw [it], he answered unto the people, Ye men of Israel, why marvel ye at this? or why look ye so earnestly on us, as though by our own power or holiness we had made this man to walk?

:13 The God of Abraham, and of Isaac, and of Jacob, the God of our fathers, hath glorified his Son Jesus; whom ye delivered up, and denied him in the presence of Pilate, when he was determined to let [him] go.

:14 But ye denied the Holy One and the Just, and desired a murderer to be granted unto you;

:15 And killed the Prince of life, whom God hath raised from the dead; whereof we are witnesses.

:16 And his name through faith in his name hath made this man strong, whom ye see and know: yea, the faith which is by him hath given him this perfect soundness in the presence of you all.

:17 And now, brethren, I wot that through ignorance ye did [it], as [did] also your rulers.

:18 But those things, which God before had showed by the mouth of all

The ten horns, (the rulers of Rome), together with the seven heads, (an alliance of Rome and Israel), are also mentioned in connection with the dragon and the beast on which the woman sat.

Rev 12:3 And there appeared another wonder in heaven; and behold a great red dragon, having seven heads and ten horns, and seven crowns upon his heads.

:1 And I stood upon the sand of the sea, and saw a beast rise up out of the sea, having seven heads and ten horns, and upon his horns ten crowns, and upon his heads the name of blasphemy.

Heads are rulers, or people in high authority. The Roman rulers joined the Jewish rulers against the Messiah, forming these seven heads. The book of Revelation, chapter seventeen, symbolically refers to them as mountains.

Rev 17:9 And here [is] the mind which hath wisdom. The seven heads are seven mountains, on which the woman sitteth.

In Daniel chapter nine, seventy weeks were determined on Daniel's people and city, which would lead to the revealing of the Messiah. Tiberius was the third Caesar in Rome, and in his 15th year of reigning, John came baptizing people unto repentance, preparing the way for the Christ.

This was a very important time in history. The stage was set for the greatest event ever on the face of planet earth. Jesus was baptized by John and it marked the beginning of his ministry, as well as the beginning of the last week, of the seventy-week prophecy in Daniel chapter nine. The rulers of the world, the seven heads of the dragon, were also in place.

All this is found in the word. Scripture must explain scripture. The only history that can explain scripture is the history that took place during the writing of that certain text. The whole of the New Testament was written during the time of Rome rule. Modern history cannot be used to explain things that happened during the Roman rule.

Bible history can be used for spiritual applications, but it cannot change the historical facts. The Word is given by the Spirit and the Spirit will never lead you where the Word cannot sustain it. THE WORD IS FOREVER SETTLED IN THE HEAVENS. We have no right to change or impose our natural interpretation of the Word on others.

It is your duty as a Christian to;

> **1 Ti 4:16** Take heed unto thyself, and unto the doctrine; continue in them: for in doing this thou shalt both save thyself, and them that hear thee.

> **2 Ti 2:15** Study to shew thyself approved unto God, a workman

that needeth not to be ashamed, rightly dividing the word of truth.

SATAN AND HIS TEAM HAD ONE COMMON PURPOSE AND THAT WAS TO STOP THE SEED.

1 Cor 2:7 But we speak the wisdom of God in a mystery, [even] the hidden [wisdom], which God ordained before the world unto our glory:

:8 Which none of the princes of this world knew: for had they known [it], they would not have crucified the Lord of glory.

Luke chapter three is an amazing chapter. It covers the year 27AD, the fifteenth year of Tiberius Caesar. This chapter reveals the seven heads described in Revelation and fits the timing of the seventy week prophesy, of Daniel nine.

Seventy weeks of years were determined upon the people and the city unto their Messiah. This period is broken up in 7 weeks and 62 weeks, that gives us 69 weeks or 483 years. The countdown started when the command to rebuild Jerusalem went forth. This command went forth in the year 457 BC with Artaxerxes. Making the calculations we come to 27AD.

483-457 AD = 26BC   We have to ad one year for the turn of the century. That brings us to 27 AD, the year Jesus was baptized, to fulfil all righteousness. The stage was set and Jesus was inaugurated from heaven.

This all comes together in Luke three;

Luke 3:1 IN THE fifteenth year of

1. Tiberius Caesar's reign-when
2. Pontius Pilate was governor of Judea, and
3. Herod was tetrarch of Galilee, and his brother
4. Philip tetrarch of the region of Ituraea and Trachonitis, and
5. Lysanias tetrarch of Abilene-

Luke 3:2 In the high priesthood of

6. Annas and
7. Caiaphas,

the Word of God [concerning the attainment through Christ of salvation in the kingdom of God] came to John son of Zachariah in the wilderness (desert).

Luke 3:3 And he went into all the country round about the Jordan, preaching a baptism of repentance for the remission of sins;

Here, the seven heads are revealed and players are in place, for the battle of the ages. The first ones that came to be baptized by John, were the carriers of serpent seed.

Luke 3:7 Then said he to the multitude that came forth to be baptized of him, O generation of vipers, who hath warned you to flee from the wrath to come?

3. THE DRAGON

There is no doubt as to who the Dragon is. The serpent of the book of Genesis has grown in stature and is now called; "the Old Serpent", the Dragon. He is described as having ten horns and seven heads.

Rev 12:3 And there appeared another wonder in heaven; and behold a great red dragon, having seven heads and ten horns, and seven crowns upon his heads.

There is very little revealed in the Word of the origin of Satan. Peter tells us about angels that sinned. This event is not at all recorded in the Bible and it is generally assumed that this rebellion of the angels took place before the age of the existence of the human race.

> **2 Pet 2:4** … God spared not the angels that sinned, but cast [them] down to hell, and delivered [them] into chains of darkness, to be reserved unto judgment;

> **Jude 1:6** And the angels which kept not their first estate, but left their own habitation, he hath reserved in everlasting chains under darkness unto the judgment of the great day.

We do however, know more about his working. Satan first deceives people and then accuses them, but he lost the seat or place of accusation and was totally stripped of power, since Jesus took all sin upon Himself and overcame evil with good, through His death.

> **1 John 3:8** …For this purpose the Son of God was manifested, that he might destroy the works of the devil.

The Kingdom of God, which is from Heaven, was now brought to earth in and by Christ. Satan had his last attempt to ultimately destroy the seed, the infant church. This is when persecution and tribulation broke loose like never before.

Daniel had visions of these times and God commanded him to seal it. These seals were broken when the lamb was slain and the wrath poured out on that generation that called for His blood on them and their children.

It has nothing to with the time we live in, or the end of the earth. It was the end of that world, that generation that rejected the Christ.

> **Dan 10:1** IN THE third year of Cyrus king of Persia a word was revealed to Daniel, who was called Belteshazzar. And the word was true and it referred to great tribulation (conflict and wretchedness). And he understood the word and had understanding of the vision.

This was the third Massacre in the seed line of salvation.
1. The Babies in Moses Time
2. The Babies in the time of Christ
3. The Tribulation on the infant Church.

Satan was bound a thousand years. The word "Millennium", is not in the Bible. Thousand years means; "PERFECT TIME". The only perfect time on earth was when Satan was not able to kill. Jesus took the temptation for every man and Satan left for a more opportune season. Jesus and Satan were bound a thousand years, a perfect time. Satan could not kill the Christ.

Satan was loosed out of the pit when Christ gave himself over to taste death for every man, by his own choice. Satan knew his time was short and the angels cried Woe to the inhabitants of the earth and

Satan did all he could to prevent the church to be born.

The harlot system now rides the Beast, empowered and inspired by the Dragon, Satan the serpent, to destroy the church. Revelation nineteen reveals this war in the heavens.

The Rider on a White Horse is the most beautiful picture of the victory that Christ brought for the church, to the church and with the church.

> **Rev 19:11** And I saw heaven opened, and behold a white horse; and he that sat upon him was called Faithful and True, and in righteousness he doth judge and make war.
>
> :12 His eyes were as a flame of fire, and on his head were many crowns; and he had a name written, that no man knew, but he himself.
>
> :13 And he was clothed with a vesture dipped in blood: and his name is called The Word of God.
>
> :14 And the armies which were in heaven followed him upon white horses, clothed in fine linen, white and clean.
>
> :15 And out of his mouth goeth a sharp sword, that with it he should smite the nations: and he shall rule them with a rod of iron: and he treadeth the winepress of the fierceness and wrath of Almighty God.
>
> :16 And he hath on his vesture and on his thigh a name written, KING OF KINGS, AND LORD OF LORDS.
>
> :17 And I saw an angel standing in the sun; and he cried with a loud voice, saying to all the fowls that fly in the midst of heaven, Come and gather yourselves together unto the supper of the great God;
>
> :18 That ye may eat the flesh of kings, and the flesh of captains,

and the flesh of mighty men, and the flesh of horses, and of them that sit on them, and the flesh of all men, both free and bond, both small and great.

:19 And I saw the beast, and the kings of the earth, and their armies, gathered together to make war against him that sat on the horse, and against his army.

Instead of the destroying the infant church, life burst forth and the gospel spread to every corner of the known world. Satan himself, became the instrument of total destruction by taking out that old system of worship in order for the new to be established.

Psa 2:4 He that sitteth in the heavens shall laugh: the Lord shall have them in derision.

• THE ROD OF IRON

Rome was represented by Iron, from Daniel's interpretation of Nebuchadnezzar's dream. Satan was preparing himself for battle and he empowered the beast with the ten horns, Rome.

Israel allied with Rome to take out the Messiah, but just like Haman who hanged on his own gallows, Rome turned on Israel. Rome became the "Rod of Iron" in God's hand, ruling the nations and took out and destroyed the Harlot, the false prophet that was riding the Beast.

Rev 17:16 And the ten horns (kings) which thou sawest upon the beast, these shall hate the whore, and shall make her desolate and naked, and shall eat her flesh, and burn her with fire.

God ruled them with a ROD OF IRON.

> **Rev 2:27** And he shall rule them with a rod of iron; as the vessels of a potter shall they be broken to shivers: even as I received of my Father.

> **Psa 2:9** Thou shalt break them with a rod of iron; thou shalt dash them in pieces like a potter's vessel.

SATAN STIRRED JUDAISM TO USE ROME TO TAKE OUT THE CHRIST.
GOD USED ROME TO REMOVE JUDAISM,
THAT OLD SYSTEM OF WORSHIP THAT BECAME AN ABOMINATION AND
DEALT WITH SATAN AT THE SAME TIME.

God overcame evil and has not given us a spirit of fear. Satan is the loser and does not have the last say. The book of Revelation is not about Satan and His friends but about Jesus Christ, who is "the Rider on the White Horse," the ultimate Victorious One.

• THE WAR

In Revelation twelve, we find two wonders in heaven.

1. A child being born.

Rev 12:1 And there appeared a great wonder in heaven; a woman clothed with the sun, and the moon under her feet, and upon her head a crown of twelve stars:

:2 And she being with child cried, travailing in birth, and pained to be delivered.

2. Dragon that wants to destroy the child.

Rev 12:3 And there appeared another wonder in heaven; and behold a great red dragon, having seven heads and ten horns, and seven crowns upon his heads.

:4 And his tail drew the third part of the stars of heaven, and did cast them to the earth: and the dragon stood before the woman which was ready to be delivered, for to devour her child as soon as it was born.

Satan was cast out of heaven by Michael. The accuser lost his seat of accusation in heaven and he was cast down to the earth.

Rev 12:7 And there was war in heaven: Michael and his angels fought against the dragon; and the dragon fought and his angels,

:8 And prevailed not; neither was their place found any more in heaven.

:9 And the great dragon was cast out, that old serpent, called the Devil, and Satan, which deceiveth the whole world: he was cast out into the earth, and his angels were cast out with him.

:10 And I heard a loud voice saying in heaven, Now is come salvation, and strength, and the kingdom of our God, and the power of his Christ: for the accuser of our brethren is cast down, which accused them before our God day and night.

This was also revealed to Daniel by the angel Gabriel;

> **Dan 12:1** And at that time shall Michael stand up, the great prince which standeth for the children of thy people: and there shall be a time of trouble, such as never was since there was a nation [even] to that same time: and at that time thy people shall be delivered, every one that shall be found written in the book.

The Word explains the Word and you cannot read Revelation without the rest of the Word.

• THE TEMPTATION

Satan knew, he had a little time and he went full out, trying to destroy the seed. Jesus fulfilled all righteousness at His baptism and was deliberately led into the desert, by the Spirit. There, in the heat of the desert, He was tempted of Satan on His Sonship and passed the tests that Adam failed in the cool of the garden.

> **1 Cor 10:13** There hath no temptation taken you but such as is common to man:
> **1 John 2:16** For all that [is] in the world,
> 1. the lust of the flesh, and
> 2. the lust of the eyes, and
> 3. the pride of life, is not of the Father, but is of the world.
> **1 John 2:17** And the world passeth away, and the lust thereof: but he that doeth the will of God abideth for ever.

This time, Satan's deception did not work and he left for a more opportune time, which happened to be the Cross. There, however, he met his fate once and for all.

• THE FINAL VICTORY

1 John 3:8 ... For this purpose, the Son of God was manifested, that he might destroy the works of the devil.

Jesus totally stripped Satan from His power, at the cross.

Col 2:13 And you, being dead in your sins and the uncircumcision of your flesh, hath he quickened together with him, having forgiven you all trespasses;
:14 Blotting out the handwriting of ordinances that was against us, which was contrary to us, and took it out of the way, nailing it to his cross;
:15 [And] having spoiled principalities and powers, he made a shew of them openly, triumphing over them in it.

Paul makes it quite clear that everything we have, is because of the cross.

1 Cor 2:2 For I determined not to know any thing among you, save Jesus Christ, and him crucified.

Jesus got the complete victory on the Cross, which is now passed on to everyone that would believe and to be manifested in Sonship.

Rom 8:19 For the earnest expectation of the creature waiteth for the manifestation of the sons of God.

THE REMOVAL
CHAPTER FOUR

The forty-year period, that followed the crucifixion, was a troublesome time of transition. Very little attention was given to this time in the past, because of the wrong interpretation of Bible prophecy.

Jesus totally fulfilled the Law, but the Jews held on to the Law and after they killed the Christ, they paid people to lie about His resurrection and tried to wipe out His name from the earth. This sparked terrible persecutions that spilled over in a full-time war with Rome, who in turn, became; "The Rod of Iron", in God's hands.

By killing the Christ, Israel brought the Day of Vengeance on themselves, a time period that Christ did not mention when He announced the year of favour from Isaiah's prophecy.

This didn't just happened overnight. All this was prophesied to Israel, but they killed the prophets and then wanted to escape the coming wrath, by trying to be baptized by John.

> **Luke 3:7** Then said he to the multitude that came forth to be baptized of him, O generation of vipers, who hath warned you to flee from the wrath to come?

There are so many topics found in Revelation that deals with the total fulfilment of all that was prophesied, that it sometimes side-tracks us in our understanding the essence of the book. We have to deal with some of these topics first, before looking at the seals, horses and trumpets, in order to get the whole picture.

• THE SPIRIT OF BABYLON

The Tower of Babel reflects man, exalting himself, under Satan's influence. The word Babel means confusion. Driven by Satan men tried to build a tower to reach God, but God stopped them and confounded their language. They went right on building their own small Kingdoms everywhere.

Out of the Ur of the Chaldeans, God called Abraham in order to form a nation through which he could work His plans. Abraham believed God and moved away from his family and home and lived in tents, following God. He was looking for a city, whose builder and maker is God. In Abraham God has placed a guarantee for the seed line for God.

Satan concentrated on defiling the seed line of God. He infiltrated Israel and they totally corrupted themselves and did not follow the instructions given to them, by Moses. Their downfall was unstoppable and was ignited when they rejected God, because they wanted a king. The nation went into a downward spiral which finally led to their captivity in Babylon.

> **Isa 43:14** Thus saith the LORD, your redeemer, the Holy One of Israel; For your sake I have sent to Babylon.

Babylon was later taken over by the Medes and Persians, but they inherited the spirit of Babylon. The Greek and Roman Empires formed the last two kingdoms in the statue Nebuchadnezzar dreamed about. Together these nations actually resembled the; "Image of the Beast", ruled by the spirit of Babylon. Satan was the driving power behind the Beast and Satan was preparing for the battle of the ages, between the seed of the woman and the seed of the serpent, that was ignited when Adam failed.

> **Rev 13:2** And the beast which I saw was like unto a leopard, and his feet were as [the feet] of a bear, and his mouth as the mouth of a lion: and the dragon gave him his power, and his seat, and great authority.

Satan was not only getting his camp ready, he also infiltrated and corrupted the worship system that would lead them to the Christ. Israel, not only ignored the warnings of the prophets, they killed them and in 457 BC Jerusalem was taken over by Babylon. That event only foreshadowed the burning and the total destruction of the temple.

The Ark of the Covenant disappeared during the captivity of Babylon, but they invented their own system of worship. On returning from captivity, they rebuilt the temple without an Ark behind the veil, which was now a Babylonian tapestry.

GOD WAS NOT IN IT ANYMORE.
IT WAS NOT A SYSTEM OF WORSHIP ANYMORE,
THEY NOW WORSHIPPED THE SYSTEM.

Jesus, the Messiah came to His own and was totally rejected. He had to face serpent seed within the law system, that was now totally corrupted. He made no secret of who they were.

> **Matt 23:32** Fill ye up then the measure of your fathers.
> **Matt 23:33** [Ye] serpents, [ye] generation of vipers, how can ye escape the damnation of hell?

Christ was born and crucified during the time of the Roman Empire. The temple was rebuilt by the wicked king Herod, who was appointed by Rome, and he was not even a Jew. He was also the one who massacred a whole generation, while trying to kill the baby Jesus, just like Pharaoh, in Moses' day.

Satan failed at getting rid of the seed, and now the Jewish and Roman rulers conspired together against the Christ, fulfilling David's prophecy.

> **Psa 2:2** The kings of the earth set themselves, and the rulers take counsel together, against the LORD, and against his anointed, [saying],
> :3 Let us break their bands asunder, and cast away their cords from us.

> **1 Cor 2:8** Which none of the princes of this world knew: for had they known [it], they would not have crucified the Lord of glory.

Israel's conspiracies all boomeranged in their faces. What seemed to be a defeat became the redemption plan for humanity. Christ did not destroy the law, He totally fulfilled the law and condemned sin in the flesh, by becoming the final sacrifice. He took on himself all condemnation when He was lifted up, like Moses lifted the snake in the desert, and Satan has no more power to condemn anyone. The accuser of the brethren was cast down.

> **Col 2:15** [And] having spoiled principalities and powers, he made a shew of them openly, triumphing over them in it.

> **Rom 10:4** For Christ [is] the end of the law, for righteousness to everyone that believeth.

> **Rom 8:3** For what the law could not do, in that it was weak through the flesh, God sending his own Son in the likeness of sinful flesh, and for sin, condemned sin in the flesh:

When Jesus died, He became the final sacrifice and cried; "It is finished". The earth shook and the veil in the temple was torn from top to bottom, revealing the empty holy of holies, but the Jews kept on sacrificing, not accepting the final sacrifice. They now carried the spirit of Babylon. I always wondered if they sewed the veil back together again.

Babylon is mentioned in Jesus' genealogy, and Israel's captivity in Babylon marks the beginning of their total removal, which ended in 70 A.D, when the city was destroyed and the temple burned down, by Rome, their allies in killing the Christ. God still granted them opportunity to repent over and over, but to no avail. He looked over

Jerusalem and said; "What more could have been done."

• THE REMOVAL OF THE OLD

Jesus taught that a new cloth cannot be used to fix an old garment, for both will be destroyed. He also explained that change is not always easy and people are naturally inclined to hold on to the old, rather than to receive the new. We see in his letters how Paul had to constantly deal with people wanting to go back to the old system of the law.

> **1 Cor 5:7** Purge out therefore the old leaven, that ye may be a new lump, as ye are unleavened. For even Christ our Passover is sacrificed for us:

Revelation deals with the removal of the old, and Jesus confirmed that He would finished the work He came to do. Hebrews ten is a good summary, of what the whole Bible is actually about. Paul keeps referring to the sacrifices that could not get the job done and then reveals the three-fold purpose of the coming of the Christ.

1. **Heb 10:5** Wherefore when he cometh into the world, he saith, Sacrifice and offering thou wouldest not, but a body hast thou prepared me:
2. **Heb 10:7** Then said I, Lo, I come (in the volume of the book it is written of me,) to do thy will, O God.
3. **Heb 10:9** Then said he, Lo, I come to do thy will, O God. He taketh away the first, that he may establish the second.

The Book of Revelation mostly deals with the completion of the work that was started in Babylon and climaxed on the cross; the removal of that old system.

YOU CANNOT READ REVELATION APART FROM THE REST OF THE BIBLE.

Heb 9:8 The Holy Ghost this signifying, that the way into the holiest of all was not yet made manifest, while as the first tabernacle was yet standing:

Rev 15:5 And after that I looked, and, behold, the temple of the tabernacle of the testimony in heaven was opened:

:8 And the temple was filled with smoke from the glory of God, and from his power; and no man was able to enter into the temple, till the seven plagues of the seven angels were fulfilled.

John 4:34 Jesus saith unto them, My meat is to do the will of him that sent me, and to finish his work.

- ON THE CROSS JESUS CRIED: "IT IS FINISHED". - IN REVELATION HE SAID TO JOHN: "IT IS DONE".

The final removal of the old system of worship is found in Revelation, and it took place in a definite order, as was prophesied. This forty-year period from the Crucifixion to 70 AD, deals with the direct history of that time, and it all happened to a specific generation, called; "The wicked generation".

WE ARE NOT IN THAT TIME
WE ARE NOT THAT GENERATION.
WE ARE; "THE CHRIST GENERATION".

Take Note: Revelation is full of symbolic language.

- Three is God's number,

- Four is the number for creation.

- Seven the number of God working on earth;

Revelation is full of the number seven.

- Ten means complete

- Forty is the number for a generation.

This transition from the old to the new, is divided in; three sets of seven:

1. SEVEN SEALS

2. SEVEN TRUMPETS

3. SEVEN VIALS

Every set of events had a specific purpose and was worked out in three stages.

1. On the people,

2. On the city

3. On the temple (in one day)

As the Son of Man, God dealt with man's redemption from sin, which included the removal of that old system that they clung on, so dearly.

• THE DAY OF VENGEANCE

The "Day of Vengeance" was predicted to be a day of doom and darkness. This was not a twenty-four-hour day as we know days, but it is a specific time period.

Jesus came, in the power of the Holy Spirit, from the desert into the synagogue and deliberately opened the scroll. He found and read Isaiah 61, but He left out a certain portion of this prophesy.

> **Luke 4:17** And there was delivered unto him the book of the prophet Esaias. And when he had opened the book, he found the place where it was written,
> :18 The Spirit of the Lord [is] upon me, because he hath anointed me to preach the gospel to the poor; he hath sent me to heal the brokenhearted, to preach deliverance to the captives, and recovering of sight to the blind, to set at liberty them that are bruised,
> :19 To preach the acceptable year of the Lord.
> :20 And he closed the book, and he gave [it] again to the minister, and sat down. And the eyes of all them that were in the synagogue were fastened on him.
> :21 And he began to say unto them, This day is this scripture fulfilled in your ears.

Compare this to the prophesy in Isaiah.

> **Isa 61:1** The Spirit of the Lord GOD [is] upon me; because the

LORD hath anointed me to preach good tidings unto the meek; he hath sent me to bind up the broken hearted, to proclaim liberty to the captives, and the opening of the prison to [them that are] bound;

:2 To proclaim the acceptable year of the LORD, and the day of vengeance of our God;

He came to His own, but they received Him not. Jesus was not absent minded; He gave them yet another chance to turn Totally infiltrated with serpent seed, the Jews unleashed upon themselves, "The Day of Vengeance of our God", by crucifying the Christ.

Matt 27:25 Then answered all the people, and said, His blood [be] on us, and on our children.

"The Day of Vengeance", was clearly spelled out by the prophets.

Isa 34:8 For [it is] the day of the LORD'S vengeance, [and] the year of recompenses for the controversy of Zion.

:9 And the streams thereof shall be turned into pitch, and the dust thereof into brimstone, and the land thereof shall become burning pitch.

:10 It shall not be quenched night nor day; the smoke thereof shall go up forever: from generation to generation it shall lie waste; none shall pass through it forever and ever.

This prophesy could not refer to their captivity to Babylon, as they returned and rebuilt their city as well as the temple and lived there. It referred to their final removing.

Jer 46:8 ... I will destroy the city and the inhabitants thereof.
:9 Come up, ye horses; and rage, ye chariots; and let the mighty
    men come forth:
:10 For this [is] the day of the Lord GOD of hosts, a day of
    vengeance, that he may avenge him of his adversaries: and the
    sword shall devour, and it shall be satiate and made drunk
    with their blood:

Isa 13:6 Howl ye; for the day of the LORD [is] at hand; it shall
    come as a destruction from the Almighty.

Isa 34:8 For [it is] the day of the LORD'S vengeance, [and] the year
    of recompenses for the controversy of Zion.

Isa 63:4 For the day of vengeance [is] in mine heart, and the year
    of my redeemed is come.

God's wrath was now kindled upon them, and they knew it, for they
even tried to escape from this time of wrath, by trying to be baptized
by John.

Luke 3:7 Then said he to the multitude that came forth to be
    baptized of him, O generation of vipers, who hath warned you
    to flee from the wrath to come?

Israel did not only miss their visitation, they killed the Lord of life,
and thus brought, "The day of God's Vengeance" upon themselves.

• THE SONG OF MOSES

All that happened to Israel was given to them in a song that Moses wrote and sang to them before he departed. God commanded Moses to write this song and told him that Israel would sin themselves bankrupt after his death. The song revealed that, at their latter end would be a time of devastation.

> **Deut 31:19** Now therefore write ye this song for you, and teach it the children of Israel: put it in their mouths, that this song may be a witness for me against the children of Israel.
>
> :21 And it shall come to pass, when many evils and troubles are befallen them, that this song shall testify against them as a witness;
>
> :22 Moses therefore wrote this song the same day, and taught it the children of Israel.

We just cannot read and interpret the book of Revelation without understanding and reading the entire book.

Here are just parts of the song:

> **Deut 32:5** They have corrupted themselves [they are] a perverse and crooked generation.
>
> :16 They provoked him to jealousy with strange [gods], with abominations provoked they him to anger.
>
> :20 And he said, I will hide my face from them, I will see what their end [shall be]: for they [are] a very forward generation, children in whom [is] no faith.
>
> :22 For a fire is kindled in mine anger, and shall burn unto the lowest hell, and shall consume the earth with her increase, and set on fire the foundations of the mountains.

:24 [They shall be] burnt with hunger, and devoured with burning heat, and with bitter destruction: I will also send the teeth of beasts upon them, with the poison of serpents of the dust.

:25 The sword without, and terror within, shall destroy both the young man and the virgin, the suckling [also] with the man of grey hairs.

:29 O that they were wise, [that] they understood this, [that] they would consider their latter end!

:32 For their vine [is] of the vine of Sodom, and of the fields of Gomorrah: their grapes [are] grapes of gall, their clusters [are] bitter:

:33 Their wine [is] the poison of dragons, and the cruel venom of asps.

:35 To me [belongeth] vengeance, and recompense; their foot shall slide in [due] time: for the day of their calamity [is] at hand, and the things that shall come upon them make haste.

:44 And Moses came and spake all the words of this song in the ears of the people,

John writes in Revelation; "They sang the song of Moses and the Lamb", indicating that it was the time, Moses sang about.

Rev 15:3 And they sing the song of Moses the servant of God, and the song of the Lamb, saying, Great and marvellous [are] thy works, Lord God Almighty; just and true [are] thy ways, thou King of saints.

Their latter end became the final transition from the old to the new.

• THAT GENERATION

Jesus cursed the fig tree and proclaimed that no-one would ever eat of it again, yet most people I know, have eaten figs. He was symbolically speaking about Israel that developed their own system within God's established pattern, but they had no fruit. They did things their own way, like in the garden, when they used fig leaves for coverage. That is why Jesus cursed the fig tree.

They became an abomination to God, and determined their own downfall. They went so far as killing the Christ and then cried for His blood to come on them and their children. Jesus confirmed it before He died:

> **Matt 23:36** "Verily I say unto you;all these things shall come upon this generation.
> :37 O Jerusalem, Jerusalem, thou that killest the prophets, and stonest them which are sent unto thee, how often would I have gathered thy children together, even as a hen gathereth her chickens under her wings, and ye would not!
> :38 Behold, your house is left unto you desolate.
> **Matt 24:34** Verily I say unto you, This generation shall not pass, till all these things be fulfilled.

These are the calamities that were to come upon Daniel's people, their city and their temple, at their end.(Dan 9:24). It has nothing to do with us or this age we live in.

> **Dan 12:9** And he said, Go thy, way, Daniel: for the words are closed up and sealed till the time of the end. (the end of that world)

• THE WINEPRESS

Israel was compared to the vine.

Isa 5:1 Now will I sing to my well-beloved a song of my beloved touching his vineyard. My well-beloved hath a vineyard in a very fruitful hill.

:2 And he fenced it, and gathered out the stones thereof, and planted it with the choicest vine, and built a tower in the midst of it, and also made a winepress therein: and he looked that it should bring forth grapes, and it brought forth wild grapes.

:3 And now, O inhabitants of Jerusalem, and men of Judah, judge, I pray you, betwixt me and my vineyard.

:4 What could have been done more to my vineyard, that I have not done in it? wherefore, when I looked that it should bring forth grapes, brought it forth wild grapes?

:5 And now go to; I will tell you what I will do to my vineyard: I will take away the hedge thereof, and it shall be eaten up; [and] break down the wall thereof, and it shall be trodden down:

Jesus' death also sparked the treading of the winepress and the unleashing of God's wrath. Jesus trod the winepress, which marked the end of that specific harvest, the harvest of grapes.

Rev 14:19 And the angel thrust in his sickle into the earth, and gathered the vine of the earth, and cast [it] into the great winepress of the wrath of God.

Rev 19:15 And out of his mouth goeth a sharp sword, that with it he should smite the nations: and he shall rule them with a rod of iron: and he treadeth the winepress of the fierceness and wrath of Almighty God.

Isa 63:3 I have trodden the winepress alone; and of the people [there was] none with me: for I will tread them in mine anger, and trample them in my fury; and their blood shall be sprinkled upon my garments, and I will stain all my raiment.

The cross ignited the treading of the winepress. God took Israel out, and in doing so, gave them a new chance, "In Christ". We cannot go back or hold on to what was broken down, no matter who teaches it. We now, have to hear what the Spirit says.

Gal 2:18 For if I build again the things which I destroyed, I make myself a transgressor.

Gal 2:21 I do not frustrate the grace of God: for if righteousness [come] by the law, then Christ is dead in vain.

Christ the rider on the white horse, ruled with a Rod of Iron, treading the wine press. This is so different than what I was taught.

• SODOM AND GOMORRAH

Israel now became what they worshipped. Moses predicted before his death, that Israel would be as Sodom and Gomorrah to God.

Deut 29:22 So that the generation to come of your children that shall rise up after you, and the stranger that shall come from afar land, shall say, when they see the plagues of that land, and the sicknesses which the LORD hath laid upon it;

:23 [And that] the whole land thereof [is] brimstone, and salt, [and] burning, [that] it is not sown, nor beareth, nor any grass growth therein, like the overthrow of Sodom, and Gomorrah, Admah, and Zeboim, which the LORD overthrew in his anger, and in his wrath:

This was also confirmed by the prophets, before their captivity.

Jer 23:14 I have seen also in the prophets of Jerusalem a horrible thing: they commit adultery, and walk in lies: they strengthen also the hands of evildoers, that none doth return from his wickedness: they are all of them unto me as Sodom, and the inhabitants thereof as Gomorrah.

Sodom and Gomorrah foreshadowed what was to come on Israel and finally to all unbelievers.

Rev 11:8 …the great city, which spiritually is called Sodom and Egypt, where also our Lord was crucified.

• THE ABOMINATION

This word appears over one hundred times in the Old Testament and a few times in the New Testament.

Matt 24:15 When ye therefore shall see the abomination of desolation, spoken of by Daniel the prophet, stand in the holy place, (whoso readeth, let him understand:)

:16 Then let them which be in Judaea flee into the mountains:

Antiochus Epiphanes, from the Seleucid Empire (Hellenistic Greeks) who ruled from 175-164BC, totally desecrated the temple by erecting a statue of Zeus and the offering of a swine on the altar. Rome was the next World Empire and they continued the hatred on the Jews, and had no respect for their religion. Rome was described in Daniel seven as a very terrible beast and many Jews lost their lives.

> **Dan 7:7** (Ampl) After this I saw in the night visions, and behold, a fourth beast [the Roman empire]-terrible, powerful and dreadful, and exceedingly strong. And it had great iron teeth; it devoured and crushed and trampled what was left with its feet. And it was different from all the beasts that came before it, and it had ten horns [symbolizing ten kings].

There were constant clashes between Romans and the Jews, and Roman rulers seemed to follow the steps of Antiochus in aggravating the Jews by defiling the temple repeatedly. Yet, when the Christ appeared, their true colours surfaced. The so-called keepers of the law now bent the law to their liking and used the law to kill the Christ. They themselves became an abomination to God.

> **John 19:7** The Jews answered him, We have a law, and by our law he ought to die, because he made himself the Son of God.

The Jews now allied with Rome, their enemy, to remove the Messiah and used the law as an excuse.

John 18:30 They answered and said unto him, If he were not a malefactor, we would not have delivered him up unto thee.

:31 Then said Pilate unto them, Take ye him, and judge him according to your law. The Jews therefore said unto him, It is not lawful for us to put any man to death:

They were masters of deception and distorted the law, to fit their cause. They recited and studied the law, yet they were blinded by their own perverseness and twisting of the law.

The law had clear guidelines.

Exo 20:16 Thou shalt not bear false witness against thy neighbour.

Luke 18:20 Thou knowest the commandments, Do not commit adultery, Do not kill, Do not steal, Do not bear false witness, Honour thy father and thy mother.

Matt 26:59 Now the chief priests, and elders, and all the council, sought false witness against Jesus, to put him to death;

:60 But found none: yea, though many false witnesses came, [yet] found they none. At the last came two false witnesses,

In the story of Esther, Haman eventually hung, on the very gallows that he prepared for Mordecai. It was foreshadowing of what was to happen to Israel. Rome, their ally, became the Rod of Iron in God's hand, that brought the final destruction to Jerusalem.

• THE TRANSITION PROCESS

The removal of that old system of worship happened systematically.
- Opening of the Seals
- Blowing of the Trumpets
- Pouring out of the Vials

The removing of the old system had already started when Israel
was taken captive in Babylon, but God commanded Daniel to seal
everything, until the time of the end.

> **Dan 9:24** Seventy weeks are determined upon thy people and
> upon thy holy city, to finish the transgression,

> **Dan 12:4** But thou, O Daniel, shut up the words, and seal the
> book, [even] to the time of the end: many shall run to and fro,
> and knowledge shall be increased.

> **Dan 12:9** And he said, Go thy way, Daniel: for the words [are]
> closed up and sealed till the time of the end.

In Revelation five, no one could be found worthy to open the book
and then the Lion out of the tribe of Judah stepped forward, the only
one found worthy to open the seals. As the Lion took the book, the
Lamb, resembling the crucified Christ, opened the seals. The four
horses or kingdoms from the time of captivity were revealed and the
rest of the persecution followed.

Four is the number for earth or creation. The four horses were also described by Zechariah chapter six.

> **Zech 6:1** four chariots out from between two mountains of brass.
> :5 And the angel answered and said unto me, These [are] the four spirits of the heavens, which go forth from standing before the Lord of all the earth.
> :6 The black horses which [are] therein go forth into the north country; and the white go forth after them; and the grisled go forth toward the south country.
> :7 And the bay went forth, and sought to go that they might walk to and fro through the earth:

The four Horses were followed by the growing intensity of the Roman persecution on the Jewish people. Rome was frustrated because unlike other territories, they just could not get full control of Jerusalem. It was a dark, turbulent period in Jewish history, famine and death, being the order of the day. There was no peace or harmony.

1. THE SEVEN SEALS

The angel Gabriel revealed to Daniel the world history that leads up to the Messiah. It was a period of four-hundred-and-ninety years. In the last chapter of Daniel, the angel commands Daniel to seal the visions and to rest with the fathers.

These seals had to be opened in the last days and we find the opening of the seals in Revelation five.

> **Rev 5:1** And I saw in the right hand of him that sat on the throne

a book written within and on the backside, sealed with seven seals.

TO SEAL,
MEANS TO PRESERVE OR TO LOCK UP.
IT MEANS THE MATTER IS KEPT SAFE.

The sealed book, in the hands of the one on the throne was written;
- on the inside; meaning what is busy happening,
- on the back; this referred to past happenings.

Daniel had to seal what he saw, until the things came to pass. The seals would not have been broken, if Israel received their day of visitation.
- John again was to write and not seal his visions.

Rev 22:10 And he saith unto me, Seal not the sayings of the prophecy of this book: for the time is at hand.

When the seals were opened it revealed four horses, which is also the four winds that came from all over the earth. They were already running. They were the four great Empires that ruled the world in succession: Babylon, Medo-Persia, Greece and Rome. The whole New Testament took place during the time of Rome.

1. The first seal, was a White Horse with a rider with a bow and a crown and He came conquering to conquer (Rev 6:2).

God revealed to Daniel that Babylon was the head of Gold from

Nebuchadnezzar's statue, which in turn resembled the, "Image of the Beast". This was the opposing force that Satan worked up to take out the Messiah. The worldly system and the kingdoms of the earth, were preparing for the great battle. They consisted of the four world empires that came in succession from the people of the earth.

The first empire to rule the whole known world was Babylon and the seals speak for themselves.

2. The second seal was a Red Horse and the rider was given a sword to take peace from the earth(Rev 6:3).

3. The third seal was a Black Horse and he that sat on him had a pair of scales in his hand, which brought in famine (Rev 6:5).

4. The fourth seal was a Pale Horse and his name that sat on him was death, and hell followed with him (Rev 6:8).

Daniel seven describes the fourth beast, as very wicked. It is during the reign of Rome that Jesus, son of God, was manifested and the book of revelation was written.

> **Dan 7:7** After this I saw in the night visions, and behold, a fourth beast [the Roman empire]-terrible, powerful and dreadful, and exceedingly strong. And it had great iron teeth; it devoured and crushed and trampled what was left with its feet. And it was different from all the beasts that came before it, and it had ten horns [symbolizing ten kings].

When the fifth seal opened, the mood changed and all the martyrs cried out and the time came for the revenge of the blood of the prophets.

5. The fifth, seal was revealing underneath the alter the souls of them that were slain for the Word of God, and for the testimony which they held- they were told to hold on yet a little while(Rev 6:9).

The sixth seal describe the crucifixion and announced the "Day of Gods Vengeance". After the crucifixion, the persecution of Christians started by the Sanhedrin. Rome did not like the upheaval and they then turned on the Jews with persecution. First it came down upon the people, then their city and finally on their temple.

6. When the sixth seal was opened, there was a great earthquake; the sun became black as sackcloth of hair, and the moon became as blood; and the stars of heaven fell unto the earth, even as a fig tree cast her untimely figs, when she is shaken of a mighty wind. And the heaven departed as a scroll. (Rev 6:12)

The sun, moon and stars are all symbolic language that pointed to Judaism. Joseph dreamed of the sun, moon and stars bowing; here John saw them falling. The fig tree symbolized man doing things his own way, from the garden, when they used fig leaves to cover their nakedness. The fig tree is that counterfeit religious system, that infiltrated Judaism, it literally means; I'll do it my way. That is also the reason Jesus cursed the fig tree.
The worst announcement ever made, is found in Revelation six.

Rev 6:15 And the kings of the earth, and the great men, and the rich men, and the chief captains, and the mighty men, and every bondman, and every free man, hid themselves in the dens and in the rocks of the mountains;

:16 And said to the mountains and rocks, Fall on us, and hide us from the face of him that sitteth on the throne, and from the wrath of the Lamb:

:17 For the great day of His wrath is come; and who shall be able to stand?

This marked the point where the Jewish system collapsed and there was no more order. The seventh seal was about to be broken and John saw four angels, holding the four winds, until the 144000 were sealed on their foreheads.

Three is the number for God and four is earth's number

> 3x4=12 God working on the earth, His governing number.
> 10 = completion and ten to the power of three, perfection
> 10x10x10 =1000= perfection

144000 =12x12x 100= All God's people in the old and the new.

God protected the ones who kept His Word and warned them in Matthew twenty-four to flee Jerusalem. The Christians, who had obeyed, were the ones who survived the day of calamity and destruction.

7. **Rev 8:1** And when he had opened the seventh seal, there was

silence in heaven about the space of half an hour.

Rev 8:2 And I saw the seven angels which stood before God; and to them were given seven trumpets.

The seventh seal sparked the blowing of the seven trumpets.

2. THE SEVEN TRUMPETS

By the time Jesus appeared on the scene, Israel was desperately in need of a Saviour, because life was unbearable under Roman oppression. Rome ultimately wanted their city, Jerusalem and the Jews received no mercy from Rome.

The persecution grew in intensity and the abomination set up in the temple by Caligula around 41 AD sparked the last revolt, that in turn, led to Rome surrounding Jerusalem with ten legions of soldiers in 66 AD, under the command of Titus, the son of Vespasian, the new Emperor of Rome.

The trumpets blowing were the unleashing of destruction and calamity upon the city. Jerusalem was totally cut off from the outside world and no-one could enter or leave the city. If they dared to leave they were crucified. Josephus recorded that the hills outside Jerusalem were covered with crosses as far as the eye could see and the stench was unbearable.
On the inside, the city was divided in three factions, under three

Zealot fighters: Simon and John of Giscala, and the high priest, Eleazar.

> **Rev 16:19** And the great city was divided into three parts, and the cities of the nations fell: and great Babylon came in remembrance before God, to give unto her the cup of the wine of the fierceness of his wrath.

These men worked up a greater war inside the city, than what was going on outside. More people were killed on the inside. They forced everybody to take part in the fighting within, or they would be killed anyway. Bodies were lying as high as the horses' bridles in the streets of Jerusalem. Pestilence and famine was the order of the day. People were running on the walls of the city screaming at the Romans for help, asking if someone could bring peace to the city.

When the Romans attacked, the Jews turned as one against them and then resumed the inside fighting again and then the Roman armies backed off. These three factions destroyed the city from within, and every time a trumpet sounded a third part, one faction, was hurt. This all happened inside the city. Daniel described it as a time of trouble; such as never was, since there was a nation:

THE BATTLE FOR POWER WAS WITHIN AND WITHOUT. THIS WAS ALSO FOUND IN THE SONG OF MOSES.

> **Deut 32:25** The sword without, and terror within, shall destroy both the young man and the virgin, the suckling [also] with the man of gray hairs.

FIRST TRUMPET -**Rev 8:7** - hail and fire mingled with blood fell on earth, the third part of trees was burnt up, and all green grass was burnt up.

SECOND TRUMPET- **Rev 8:8** - a great mountain burning with fire was cast into the sea: and the third part of the sea became blood and was destroyed.

Remember;
Sea refers to nations and mountains.
Trees refer to people.

THIRD TRUMPET - **Rev 8:10** - a great star called wormwood fell from heaven, upon the third part of the rivers, and they were made bitter.

Wormwood, meaning bitter and the rivers different flows of peoples and Israel was suppose to be the stars.

FOURTH TRUMPET - **Rev 8:12** -And the fourth angel sounded, and the third part of the sun, moon and stars were smitten,

The sun, moon and stars are the heavenly elements and refer to Israel.
Rev 8:13 Then the angels started crying; "Woe, woe, woe, to the inhabitants of the earth", by reason of the three angels, which are yet to sound!

THE FIFTH TRUMPET announced the starting of the "Woe's"

that was announced by Jesus in Matthew 23, "Woe to you Scribes, Pharisees hypocrites." Isaiah also uses this word, concerning Israel, in it's beginning chapters,.

> **Matt 23:13** But woe unto you, scribes and Pharisees, hypocrites! for ye shut up the kingdom of heaven against men: for ye neither go in [yourselves], neither suffer ye them that are entering to go in.

> **Dan 12:1** ... and there shall be a time of trouble, such as never was since there was a nation [even] to that same time: ...

• THE THREE WOES'

1.   THE FIRST WOE: **Rev 9:1** And the fifth angel sounded, and I saw a star fall from heaven unto the earth: and to him was given the key of the bottomless pit.

2.   THE SECOND WOE: The sixth trumpet released four Angels and the persecution intensified, yet the people did not turn to God. Rev 10:7 But in the days of the voice of the seventh angel, when he shall begin to sound, the mystery of God should be finished, as he hath declared to his servants the prophets.
THE MYSTERIES OF GOD in the Word, tell their own story:

The mystery that was kept secret since the world began
    Col 1:26/Eph 3:9/Rom 16:25
  - The mystery of the wisdom of God- 1 Cor 15:51

- The mystery of the blindness of Israel- Rom 11:25
- The mystery of God's will- Eph 1:9
- The mystery of the Gospel- Eph 6 :19
- The mystery of Christ- Eph3:9/Col 4:3
- The mystery of the faith- 1 Tim 3:9
- The mystery of God the Father and Christ- Col 2:2
- The mystery of the Kingdom- Mark 4:4/Matt 13:11
- The mystery of iniquity- 2 Thess 2:7
- The mystery of the Seven Stars- Rev 1:20
- The mystery of the Woman- Rev 17:7
- The mystery of Babylon the great- Rev 17:7

Rev 11:13 And the same hour was there a great earthquake, and the tenth part of the city fell, and in the earthquake were slain of men seven thousand: and the remnant were affrighted, and gave glory to the God of heaven.

:14 The second woe is past; [and], behold, the third woe cometh quickly.

3.   THE THIRD WOE: Rev 11:15 And the seventh angel sounded; and there were great voices in heaven, saying, The kingdoms of this world are become [the kingdoms] of our Lord, and of his Christ; and he shall reign forever and ever.

These woes started during the revolt of 66AD, which led to the surrounding of Jerusalem by Roman legions.

3. THE SEVEN VIALS

Rome did not want to burn Jerusalem down, for they wanted to keep the city intact, for themselves. It was the greatest city in the world. The final burning down of the temple was such a terrible event, that Titus threw his hands in the air exclaiming, "This is no work of a man!". Nobody expected what happened there.

The temple was the heartbeat of their city and their worship. Literally everything centered around their worship and their temple. They even crucified Jesus, accusing Him of blaspheming against the temple. They were so blinded, that they did not recognize Him as the promised Messiah and fulfilment of the temple.

The temple was last to go, but it was the quickest work, in ONE DAY. It happened in such a way no one could stop it. It was such a big blow that it brought an end to Judaism. Titus finally found a way into the city by making an opening in the wall. Titus commanded the soldiers to preserve the temple, the gold was there and it was the big treasure that made this city so valuable.

On the inside fierce fighting broke out and they could not retreat. A soldier in panic set flame to the temple to distract the Jews and it went totally out of control. The fighting ceased and before everyone's eyes the temple was totally destroyed. Josephus wrote that Titus threw his hands in the air and declared that it could not be the work of a man's hands, for it looked like sulphur fell from the sky, like in Sodom.

Isa 9:14 Therefore the LORD will cut off from Israel head and tail, branch and rush, in one day.

Isa 10:17 And the light of Israel shall be for a fire, and his Holy One for a flame: and it shall burn and devour his thorns and his briers in one day;

Isa 47:9 But these two [things] shall come to thee in a moment in one day, the loss of children, and widowhood:

When the temple was touched, the heart of Judaism was touched. The vials on the temple destroyed their existence, but the voice came from the temple that called for the vials.

Rev 16:1 And I heard a great voice out of the temple saying to the seven angels, Go your ways, and pour out the vials of the wrath of God upon the earth.

1.   Rev 16:2 upon the earth; and there fell a noisome and grievous sore upon the men which had the mark of the beast, and [upon] them which worshipped his image.

2.   Rev 16:3 upon the sea; and it became as the blood of a dead [man]: and every living soul died in the sea.

3.   Rev 16:4 …the rivers and fountains of waters; and they became blood.:6 For they have shed the blood of saints and prophets, and thou hast given them blood to drink; for they are worthy.

Rev 16:7 Almighty, true and righteous [are] thy judgments.

4.   Rev 16:8 upon the sun; and power was given to scorch men

with fire. They repented not to give him glory.

5.   **Rev 16:10** upon the seat of the beast; and his kingdom was full of darkness; and they gnawed their tongues for pain.

Rev 16:11 ....and they repented not of their deeds.

The destruction of the temple was the completion of the work that the Son of man came to do. His death on the cross, down to the burning of the temple, is one action. It was the removal of that old system.

Heb 10:9 Then said he, Lo, I come to do thy will, O God. He taketh away the first, that he may establish the second.

IT IS DONE

The next two verses describe the spirits that were at work.

6.   **Rev 16:12** And the sixth angel poured out his vial upon the great river Euphrates; and the water thereof was dried up, that the way of the kings of the east might be prepared.
Rev 16:13 And I saw three unclean spirits like frogs [come] out of the mouth of the dragon and out of the mouth of the beast, and out of the mouth of the false prophet.

The last part of chapter sixteen, describes the;"Thief in the night", "Armageddon" and the calamity that followed, as well as the city that was divided and calls it "Babylon that has fallen". Remember Spirit is not bound by time, this is all explained as one period.

7.   **Rev 16:17** And the seventh angel poured out his vial into the air; and there came a great voice out of the temple of heaven, from the throne, saying, It is done.

Israel sinned themselves bankrupt, but God took Israel back, time and again. He gave her warnings upon warnings, but they were like the ten foolish virgins. On the cross Jesus died and broke covenant with Israel. Now, her judgement has come, for it had to be dealt with legally, fulfilling all the prophets decreed.

> **Rev 17:1** And there came one of the seven angels which had the seven vials, and talked with me, saying unto me, Come hither; I will shew unto thee the judgment of the great whore that sitteth upon many waters:
>
> **Rev 21:9** And there came unto me one of the seven angels which had the seven vials full of the seven last plagues, and talked with me, saying, Come hither, I will shew thee the bride, the Lamb's wife.

• BABYLON THE GREAT IS FALLEN

You become what you worship. Israel worshipped gods that could not see or hear. Even though they were the heirs of all the promises and covenants and recited the Holy Word, they could not see, and they could not hear.

> **Matt 23:37** O Jerusalem, Jerusalem, [thou] that killest the prophets, and stonest them which are sent unto thee, how

often would I have gathered thy children together, even as a hen gathereth her chickens under [her] wings, and ye would not!

In the book of Revelation chapter eleven, Jerusalem resembles Egypt and Sodom. In chapters seventeen and eighteen, the city is called Babylon and Israel resembles a great whore sitting on many waters, (Rev 17:1) and riding the beast.(Rev 17:3)

Rev 17:6 And I saw the woman drunken with the blood of the saints, and with the blood of the martyrs of Jesus: and when I saw her, I wondered with great admiration.

ISRAEL NOW RESEMBLED BABYLON.

Rev 18:2 And he cried mightily with a strong voice, saying, Babylon the great is fallen…

Rev 18:9 And the kings of the earth, who have committed fornication and lived deliciously with her, shall bewail her, and lament for her, when they shall see the smoke of her burning.

History is clear; Babylon never burned. Babylon was deserted under the Syrians, and a new capital was chosen in Assyria. Jerusalem carried the spirit of Babylon and it was burned down to the ground by Rome, the ROD of IRON, that represented Babylon.

Rev 19:3 And again they said, Alleluia. And her smoke rose up forever and ever.

Immediately the attention is turned back, in chapter nineteen, to the RIDER ON THE WHITE HORSE, whose name is the WORD, the ultimate victorious One.

NOW
THE KINGDOM OF HEAVEN
IS OPEN
TO ALL WHO WILL COME.

THE KINGDOM
CHAPTER FIVE:

John 18:36
Jesus answered, My kingdom is not of this world:
if my kingdom were of this world, then would my servants fight,
that I should not be delivered to the Jews:
but now is my kingdom not from hence.

It is very clear in the Gospel of John that the Kingdom is a world, which came into existence within this world, and it will never end.

> **John 17:14** I have given them thy word; and the world hath hated them, because they are not of the world, even as I am not of the world.
> :15 I pray not that thou shouldest take them out of the world, but that thou shouldest keep them from the evil.

When I attended Bible school, we had to have a book titled; "God's Plan for Man." This theology book was compulsory and it was about three times thicker than the Bible itself, yet to my knowledge, very few students ever read it, and those that did, was lost amongst human reasoning.

Ironically, we were told to be cautious of the book of Revelation for it would bring confusion. That intrigued me, and I started reading the book and have never stopped.

The first thing I found was a promise of blessing.

> **Rev 1:3** Blessed [is] he that readeth, and they that hear the words of this prophecy, and keep those things which are written therein`: for the time [is] at hand.

The last thing I found was a serious warning, not to put your own interpretation to this book;

> **Rev 22:18** For I testify unto every man that heareth the words of the prophecy of this book, If any man shall add unto these things, God shall add unto him the plagues that are written in this book:
> :19 And if any man shall take away from the words of the book of this prophecy, God shall take away his part out of the book of life, and out of the holy city, and [from] the things which are written in this book.

Clearly the book is very important, and man was not to tamper with its content. It contains;

"GOD'S PLAN FOR MAN";
THE KINGDOM OF GOD ON EARTH.

The last two chapters describe the Kingdom and it is clear that Satan does not have the last say. For too long Satan has ruled the minds of Christians through his lies; imposing fear upon them. Death is the root of all fear.

2 Tim 1:7 For God hath not given us the spirit of fear; but of power, and of love, and of a sound mind.

In Revelation we find the cleaning up process of the perversion of the second world, by fire. In Noah's day, the first world was cleansed with water. Water and fire, the two life giving elements, became the elements of destruction.

2 Pet 3:6 Whereby the world that then was, being overflowed with water, perished:
:7 But the heavens and the earth, which are now, by the same word are kept in store, reserved unto fire against the day of judgment and perdition of ungodly men.

The destruction of the second world, lead us into the third and final world, the world without end. The kingdom of God is that world where water and fire does not have any effect.

Isa 43:2 When thou passest through the waters, I will be with thee; and through the rivers, they shall not overflow thee: when thou walkest through the fire, thou shalt not be burned; neither shall the flame kindle upon thee.

Eph 3:20 Now unto him that is able to do exceeding abundantly above all that we ask or think, according to the power that worketh in us,
:21 Unto him be glory in the church by Christ Jesus throughout all ages, world without end. Amen.

• FROM THE BEGINNING

Deeply rooted on the inside of man, there is this mystical knowing that we are not supposed to die, but is seem that man can just not get hold of life.

> **Ecc 3:11** He hath made every thing beautiful in his time: also he hath set the world (eternity Ampl.) in their heart, so that no man can find out the work that God maketh from the beginning to the end.

In trying to find life and purpose, we actually exchange life for existing; destroying the greatest gift we have; LIFE itself. This story plays out right in front of us, yet we stay oblivious to truth. It takes a lifetime for man to find himself and just as man has seemed to reach his goals, life itself, fades. Ironically only the things received from the Spirit realm, is eternal. Now remains faith, hope and love (1 Cor 13:13).

Fear of death is the underlying reason for all superstitions and religions. It is amazing to see what people have done to preserve life. Every day new discoveries are being made of how people tried to mummify their dead, because they are trying to preserve life. Some were buried with all their possessions, only to be visited by tomb raiders. One emperor of China was buried with replicas of his whole army, the terracotta army, in order to protect him in the afterlife. Only in God there is life and immortality, their possessions did nothing for them in their afterlife, it only enriched those wise enough to find out how to break into those tombs.

1 Ti 6:16 God, who only hath immortality, dwelling in the light which no man can approach unto; whom no man hath seen, nor can see: to whom be honour and power everlasting. Amen.

Real life is only found in God. IN the beginning was the Word and in HIM was Life, and that LIFE was the LIGHT of men. This life in the Spirit, was brought to man through Christ; THE ONLY WAY.
God wanted us to live and have real life from the beginning, and His plan has never changed. In revelation God reveals and confirms that he is the beginning and the end. What He has purposed will come to pass.

Rev 1:8 I am Alpha and Omega, the beginning and the ending, saith the Lord, which is, and which was, and which is to come, the Almighty.

Rev 3:14 And unto the angel of the church of the Laodiceans write; These things saith the Amen, the faithful and true witness, the beginning of the creation of God;

Rev 21:6 And he said unto me, It is done. I am Alpha and Omega, the beginning and the end. I will give unto him that is athirst of the fountain of the water of life freely.

Rev 22:13 I am Alpha and Omega, the beginning and the end, the first and the last.

In the beginning, the Spirit hovered over the water and in the end, the Spirit, now on the inside of man, cries for the eternal unity and life in and with God.

Rev 22:17 And the Spirit and the bride say, Come. And let him that heareth say, Come. And let him that is athirst come. And whosoever will, let him take the water of life freely.

\-   **Genesis** was written by a vision given to Moses, when he requested to see God's Glory. Moses lived more or less two-thousand-five-hundred years after Adam.

\-   **Revelation** was written because of a vision given to John on the isle of Patmos. John lived about one thousand-six-hundred years after Moses.

The similarities in these books are not a coincidence. It reveals God's unchangeable purpose for man. Paul explains this in a very simple way.

Heb 10:7 Then said I, Lo, I come (in the volume of the book it is written of me,) to do thy will, O God.

Let's take a look at these two visions, given by the Spirit of God.

REVELATION ;

Rev 21:1 And I saw a new **heaven and a new earth**: for the first heaven and the first earth were passed away; and there was no more sea.

:2 And I John saw the holy city, new Jerusalem, coming down from God out of heaven, prepared as a **bride** adorned for her husband.

:3 And I heard a great voice out of heaven saying, Behold, the tabernacle of God is with men, and **He will dwell with them,** and they shall be his people, and God himself shall be with them, and be their God.

:7 He that overcometh shall inherit all things; and I will be his God, and **he shall be my son**.

:5 And he that sat upon the throne said, Behold, I make all things new. And he said unto me, Write: for these words are true and faithful.

:6 And he said unto me, It is done. I am Alpha and Omega, the **beginning and the end**. I will give unto him that is athirst of the fountain of the **water of life** freely.

Rev 22:1 And he shewed me a pure **river of water of life**, clear as crystal, proceeding out of the throne of God and of the Lamb.

:2 In the midst of the street of it, and on either side of the river, was there the **tree of life**, which bare twelve manner of fruits, and yielded her fruit every month: and the leaves of the tree were for the healing of the nations.

:3 And there shall be **no more curse**: but the throne of God and of the Lamb shall be in it; and his servants shall serve him:

:4 And they shall see his **face**; and his name shall be in their foreheads.

:5 And there shall be **no night** there; and they need no candle, neither light of the sun; for the **Lord God giveth them light**: and they shall reign for ever and ever.

GENESIS;

Gen 2:1 Thus the **heavens and the earth** were finished, and all the host of them.

:3 And God blessed the **seventh day**, and sanctified it: because that in it he had rested from all his work which God created and made.

Heb 4:9 There remaineth therefore a **rest** to the people of God.

Gen 2:7 And the LORD **God formed man** of the dust of the ground, and breathed into his nostrils the breath of life; and man became a living soul.

:8 And the LORD God planted a **garden** eastward in Eden; and there he put the man whom he had formed.

:9 And out of the ground made the LORD God to grow every **tree** that is pleasant to the sight, and good for food; **the tree of life** also in the midst of the garden, and the tree of knowledge of good and evil.

:10 And a **river** went out of Eden to water the garden; and from thence it was parted, and became into four heads.

:15 And the LORD God took the man, and put him into the garden of Eden to dress it and to keep it.

:18 And the LORD God said, It is not good that the man should be alone; I will make him an help meet for him.

Man, the image and likeness of God, now through the Spirit has access to the tree of life and the eternal kingdom of God. The Spirit that hovered in the beginning, raised Christ from the dead and now dwells in believers and leads them to what God has destined for man from the beginning.

> **Rom 8:9** But ye are not in the flesh, but in the Spirit, if so be that the Spirit of God dwell in you. Now if any man have not the Spirit of Christ, he is none of his.

> **1 Co 3:16** Know ye not that ye are the temple of God, and that the Spirit of God dwelleth in you?

He prepared us that place in the Spirit. The kingdom has come; our spirits are perfected by having God's Spirit in us and working from our inside to the perfecting of our souls, unto our final redemption.

> **1 Pe 1:9** Receiving the end of your faith, even the salvation of your souls.

> **Eph 1:14** Which is the earnest of our inheritance until the redemption of the purchased possession, unto the praise of his glory.

> **Rom 8:23** … even we ourselves groan within ourselves, waiting for the adoption, to wit, the redemption of our body.

> **Rev 22:17** And the Spirit and the bride say, Come. And let him that heareth say, Come. And let him that is athirst come. And

whosoever will, let him take the water of life freely.

SATAN DOES NOT HAVE THE LAST SAY
AND HE NEVER WILL.

• THE KINGDOM ANNOUNCED

The book of Revelation reveals the final restoration of the separation between the Creator and His Creation. It almost seems too good to be true: The Kingdom of God on earth.

1.   John the Baptist came preaching, and announced that the Kingdom is at hand.
2.   The Word became flesh, and Jesus came demonstrating and manifesting the Kingdom.
3.   Jesus sent His disciples to preach this gospel of the Kingdom to the ends of the world.

The concept of the Kingdom has been misunderstood, from the first time it was preached by Jesus Himself, to this very day. The Kingdom is not of this world, but it is in this world. It is a world, within this world, and it is not another planet somewhere beyond the blue sky.

THE KINGDOM IS
A PLACE OF PEACE JOY AND LOVE,
IN THE MIDST
OF SADNESS, UNREST AND TURMOIL.

It is a PLACE prepared;

-     This is a Place of NOW.
-     This is a place of new ways, where the old is past.
-     This is a Place of fellowship with God, indwelling your heart.
-     It is a Place of satisfaction where your thirst is quenched.
-     It is a high Place of glory, filling all emptiness.
-     This is a Place where the Heaven and earth are in agreement.
-     This is a Place permeated by God's Presence and Provision.
-     This is a Place where worship is from within.
-     This a Holy Place of peace, protection and assurance.
-     In this Place you are alive, even after you die, it is eternal.
-     This is a Place of Perfection and is symbolized by a cube. It is as long as it is wide and as deep, sealed with the bond of love.

WHAT A PLACE!

Why would anyone not want to be there? Only deception can keep anyone from wanting to be there.

I can just hear Christ's words calling through the ages:

> **Mat 24:4** ... Take heed that no man deceives you.
> **John 7:37** ..., If any man thirst, let him come unto me, and drink.

Most people postpone it until "one day" when they die, but the Kingdom has already come. This Kingdom is an above realm that is governed in truth and peace, through righteousness.

Heb 1:8 But unto the Son [he saith], Thy throne, O God, [is] for ever and ever: a sceptre of righteousness [is] the sceptre of thy kingdom.

The Kingdom of God tells us to whom it belongs.
The Kingdom of Heaven tells us what kind of kingdom it is.

OWNERSHIP AND ORIGIN.

Where is this Kingdom found?

Heaven.

Where is heaven?

Heaven was first portrayed to me as a place somewhere far, far away. It was described as a place that we would go to one day, when we die. That is not all together wrong, but it did leave an incorrect perception that heaven is a planet. A planet somewhere beyond the blue sky, where there are mansions for us to live in and some will be in shacks in the corner of Glory Land. This is not true.

Isa 66:1 Thus saith the LORD, heaven is my throne, and the earth is my footstool:

Heaven is another dimension and starts where earth ends. It is that place called "THERE" which is everywhere. It is not a place that can be worked out, or rationalised, by the human mind. Flesh and blood cannot see it, never mind entering it. The Kingdom of God, is a place in the Spirit, God's abode.

Jesus revealed the location of the heavenly realm to Nicodemus.

> **John 3:12** If I have told you earthly things, and ye believe not, how shall ye believe, if I tell you [of] heavenly things?
> :13 And no man hath ascended up to heaven, but he that came down from heaven, [even] the Son of man which is in heaven.

Jesus was standing on earth, declaring He was in heaven.

> **John 8:23** And he said unto them, Ye are from beneath; I am from above: ye are of this world; I am not of this world.

JESUS BECAME THE DOOR THAT OPENED IN HEAVEN, RIGHT HERE ON EARTH.

Jesus clearly showed that He brought Heaven within our reach. You do not have to die to enter the kingdom, you have to be born again from above.

THE NATURAL MIND CANNOT UNDERSTAND THE THINGS OF THE SPIRIT.

The spirit realm is timeless; no sun or moon is needed. There is no curse or darkness, and God is the everlasting light. It is a place of seeing, hearing and knowing. It is a higher place, an above realm, brought down to earth, a place where death is not the end.
This place is compared it to a mansion, far better than the best dwelling place on earth. This place is in the Spiritual realm that can be accessed right here on earth.

John 14:2 In my Father's house are many mansions: if [it were] not [so], I would have told you. I go to prepare a place for you.

:3 And if I go and prepare a place for you, I will come again, and receive you unto myself; that where I am, [there] ye may be also.

Jesus died and rose again and when Mary encountered Him, He would not allow her to touch Him, for He had not ascended to the Father to present His blood as an offer. Daniel talks about the Son of man entering the heavens on the clouds of heaven, before the Ancient of days and He received the Kingdom. The first time ever man entered heaven.

Dan 7:13 I saw in the night visions, and, behold, one like the Son of man came with the clouds of heaven, and came to the Ancient of days, and they brought him near before him.

:14 And there was given him dominion, and glory, and a kingdom, that all people, nations, and languages, should serve him: his dominion is an everlasting dominion, which shall not pass away, and his kingdom that which shall not be destroyed.

Later that same day, He appeared to the disciples and allowed them to touch Him, then blew over them and said "Receive the Spirit," the place prepared.

This was not the outpouring of the Spirit that empowered them. The outpouring of the Spirit came only fifty days later at Pentecost. This was the birth of the second generation man that made man capable of receiving God's Spirit and entering the Kingdom.

In Revelation one again the son of man appears on the clouds of heaven, but this time it was to finish the work that was started on the cross and it is in a total different atmosphere. The old had to be removed that the new may fully come.

> **Rev 1:7** Behold, he cometh with clouds; and every eye shall see him, and they also which pierced him: and all kindreds of the earth shall wail because of him. Even so, Amen.

• ENTERING THE KINGDOM

Nicodemus came to Jesus to find out, all by himself, the answer to the question that burned in everyone's heart. He did not want to lose favour with the religious crowd he belonged to.

> **John 3:2** Nicodemus came to Jesus by night, and said unto him, Rabbi, we know that thou art a teacher come from God: for no man can do these miracles that thou doest, except God be with him.
>
> :3 Jesus answered and said unto him, Verily, verily, I say unto thee, Except a man be born again, he cannot see the kingdom of God.
>
> :4 Nicodemus saith unto him, How can a man be born when he is old? can he enter the second time into his mother's womb, and be born?

Jesus did not answer his question, but gave him more than he was looking for. Nicodemus had no idea where this was going. Sometimes we have to really listen before we talk, this was such a time. Jesus gave him no time of day and just went on giving him what he needed.

John 3:5 Jesus answered, Verily, verily, I say unto thee, Except a man be born of water and of the Spirit, he cannot enter into the kingdom of God.

To enter the kingdom, you have to be born of water and the spirit, which is a purifying fire. This is a spiritual birth that leads to an overcoming life, in the Spirit.

Matt 3:11 I indeed baptize you with water unto repentance: but he that cometh after me is mightier than I, whose shoes I am not worthy to bear: he shall baptize you with the Holy Ghost, and with fire:

Water and fire are the two life giving elements, as well as two elements of destruction. After the fall, Adam had to till the ground and in order for seed to germinate water and energy, fire, was needed.

John 3:6 That which is born of the flesh is flesh; and that which is born of the Spirit is spirit.
:7 Marvel not that I said unto thee, Ye must be born again.
:8 The wind bloweth where it listeth, and thou hearest the sound thereof, but canst not tell whence it cometh, and whither it goeth: so is every one that is born of the Spirit.
:9 Nicodemus answered and said unto him, How can these things be?

Clearly, this ruler of the people who studied the law and the prophets, and knew the scriptures had no idea about the Spirit Life.

John 3:10 Jesus answered and said unto him, Art thou a master of

Israel, and knowest not these things?

:11 Verily, verily, I say unto thee, We speak that we do know, and testify that we have seen; and ye receive not our witness.

:12 If I have told you earthly things, and ye believe not, how shall ye believe, if I tell you of heavenly things?

The reason we can be born in the Spirit is that God Himself came and fulfilled all righteousness. God dealt with the 1st curse that came on man by removing the first sinful world with water and before the ark could land, the dove came back with an olive leave, foretelling that God's Spirit would come to fill man.

2 Pet 3:6 Whereby the world that then was, being overflowed with water, perished:

Jesus came to John, who was baptizing the people unto repentance, but He was baptized to fulfill all righteousness, submitting himself to all condemnation that was to come to man, even that of the second world, but He came to His own, and His own did not receive him, now this second world had to be dealt with.

2 Pet 3:7 But the heavens and the earth, which are now, by the same word are kept in store, reserved unto fire against the day of judgment and perdition of ungodly men.

The second world had to be destroyed with fire, because of their perverseness, but again, God took on the curse on Himself. He was baptized with fire, in that he tasted death for every man, taking on himself the second curse.

Baptism is like a burial and Paul writes to the Roman church that we must reckon ourselves dead to sin and alive to Christ. When we are baptized into His death, we are also raised with Him and the second death has no hold on us. Not even death can kill you, but His plan is for us to be manifested Sons bringing restoration to creation.

Jesus came out the water and the spirit descended on Him. John recognized Him as the lamb that was to remove the sins of the world, because the Spirit made His abode in Him.

> **John 1:33** And I knew him not: but he that sent me to baptize with water, the same said unto me, Upon whom thou shalt see the Spirit descending, and remaining on him, the same is he which baptizeth with the Holy Ghost

Our baptism in the Spirit is really the baptism of fire; it removes the wood, stubble and hay, yet we are preserved. God indented for man to receive the kingdom to the full and He himself took care of it. The Spirit is our guarantee, our down payment on our inheritance.

> **2 Co 1:22** Who hath also sealed us, and given the earnest of the Spirit in our hearts.

• THE KINGDOM HAS COME

> **Matt 18:11** For the Son of man is come to seek and save that which was lost.

Please note, Matthew uses an impersonal pronounce; "THAT", and not "THEM". Jesus brought back the kingdom and not only salvation.

The minute we are born again, it is the beginning of our journey, not the end.

The Kingdom was misunderstood right from when it was announced, because the natural man can only see in the natural. Jesus' own disciples thought that the Kingdom was to establish peace in Israel. Even after Jesus' ascension, they were still stumbling around in the dark, until they were filled with the Spirit.

We have become part of His body to manifest this kingdom on the earth. Our lives then become the road he travels.

Jesus constantly explained this glorious Kingdom, and taught his disciples to pray for the kingdom of heaven to come to earth. The Jews did not want to let go of their system of worship, for they worshipped the system and wanted the Kingdom of Israel to be restored. First they tried to crown Him as their king and when they did not get what they wanted, they then turned and crucified Him.

The progression of the revelation, of the Kingdom started with the calling of Abraham. Melchizedek served Abraham bread and wine, and it sets Abraham in the seed line of the promised redeemer. He was blessed, to be a blessing. Abraham believed God and became the father of all who believe.

Two-thousand years later, Jesus was revealed as," THE SEED"

> **John 8:56** Your father Abraham rejoiced to see my day: and he saw [it], and was glad.

Gal 3:8 And the scripture, foreseeing that God would justify the heathen through faith, preached before the gospel unto Abraham, [saying], In thee shall all nations be blessed.

Gal 3:16 Now to Abraham and his seed were the promises made. He saith not, And to seeds, as of many; but as of one, And to thy seed, which is Christ.

Four hundred-and-thirty years after the promise was given to Abraham, God's plan was revealed to Israel as a nation, but they did not believe.

Heb 4:2 For unto us was the gospel preached, as well as unto them: but the word preached did not profit them, not being mixed with faith in them that heard it.

The Passover celebration of bread and wine was set in place, the night they left Egypt. It was a matter of life and death. Those who in obedience applied the blood of the lamb to the doorposts of their dwellings, lived.

This event became an annual festival, and kept for about one thousand five hundred years, as a reminder and foreshadowing the freedom and restoration to come, in Christ.

The night Jesus was betrayed, Jesus ate the Passover meal with His disciples in Jerusalem. As they were busy eating, He revealed to them that He was to be the final sacrifice and He brought in total reformation.

Heb 10:5 Wherefore when he cometh into the world, he saith, Sacrifice and offering thou wouldest not, but a body hast thou prepared me:

He took the cup and said, "This is my Blood." Jesus then made a very important announcement;

Matt 26:29 But I say unto you, I will not drink henceforth of this fruit of the vine, until that day when I drink it new with you in my Father's kingdom.

That very moment, the last Passover meal was taken and the coming of the Kingdom, was announced.

Three days after Passover, two disciples were walking to Emmaus, when suddenly they were joined by a stranger. Despondent and sad, They talked about all that had happened in Jerusalem to Jesus, their eyes still blinded by the law, but their sorrow turned to joy.
The moment Jesus broke bread with them their eyes opened and they recognized Him. The Kingdom of heaven has now come to earth. Jesus has turned the PASSOVER INTO COMMUNION, to everyone that will believe.

Communion is now our daily portion, to remind us of the price Jesus paid and that God is building His church and not even death can kill you. We are to partake of this meal, till He comes for His Glorious, overcoming church.
The kingdom came, but the old was still a recognised institution that blocked the full receiving of the new.

REVELATION DEALS WITH
THE REMOVAL OF THE OLD.

Heb 9:8 The Holy Ghost this signifying, that the way into the holiest of all was not yet made manifest, while as the first tabernacle was yet standing:

Matt 9:16 No man putteth a piece of new cloth unto an old garment, for that which is put in to fill it up taketh from the garment, and the rent is made worse.

Rev 15:8 And the temple was filled with smoke from the glory of God, and from his power; and no man was able to enter into the temple, till the seven plagues of the seven angels were fulfilled.

These vials or plagues were poured down in the temple, and in one day it was destroyed.

Rev 16:1 And I heard a great voice out of the temple saying to the seven angels, Go your ways, and pour out the vials of the wrath of God upon the earth.

It is time to wake to this righteousness. The church, His body, was birthed and is the vehicle that brings the kingdom to this earth. What was started on the cross would never end. The Kingdom of God is forever.

Dan 7:14 And there was given him dominion, and glory, and a kingdom, that all people, nations, and languages, should serve him: his dominion [is] an everlasting dominion, which shall

not pass away, and his kingdom [that] which shall not be
destroyed.

• THE POSSESSING OF THE KINGDOM

It was revealed to Daniel that the kingdom was handed to the son of
Man who entered heaven on clouds.

> **Dan 7:13** I saw in the night visions, and, behold, one like the
> Son of man came with the clouds of heaven, and came to the
> Ancient of days, and they brought him near before him.
> :14 And there was given him dominion, and glory, and a kingdom,
> that all people, nations, and languages, should serve him: his
> dominion is an everlasting dominion, which shall not pass
> away, and his kingdom that which shall not be destroyed.

This kingdom was intended for the saints of God, the believers.

> **Dan 7:22** Until the Ancient of days came, and judgment was given
> to the saints of the most High; and the time came that the
> saints possessed the kingdom.

God wants his people to posses the Kingdom, not just to see it, but to
enter it. It was never His plan that we go in and out, in and out. No,
He wants us to possess it and to take ruler ship.

Rulership does not work without understanding authority and
authority can only function when you die to your will. Real authority
does not make claims, yet exerts real power and Jesus not only

opened the way, He is the way.

Matt 7:29 For he taught them as one having authority, and not as the scribes.

Jesus recognized it when someone understood authority and he called it faith.

Matt 8:8 The centurion answered and said, Lord, I am not worthy that thou shouldest come under my roof: but speak the word only, and my servant shall be healed.

:9 For I am a man under authority, having soldiers under me: and I say to this man, Go, and he goeth; and to another, Come, and he cometh; and to my servant, Do this, and he doeth it.

:10 When Jesus heard it, he marvelled, and said to them that followed, Verily I say unto you, I have not found so great faith, no, not in Israel.

The seat of authority in the Kingdom is very attractive to the natural, but it can only be possessed by those who walk not after the flesh. Right from the start there were those who wanted to seize the kingdom, but the sceptre of the Kingdom is righteousness, ruling within peace and joy.

Matt 11:12 And from the days of John the Baptist until now the kingdom of heaven suffereth violence, and the violent take it by force.

Matt 3:7 But when he saw many of the Pharisees and Sadducees come to his baptism, he said unto them, O generation of vipers, who hath warned you to flee from the wrath to come?

We live in a day and age where the glamour of the gospel is very attractive and focus has shifted from knowing God, to the benefits that follow believers. Being a Christian is not a formula, but a relationship, it is about knowing Him, not trying to get something or to be something.

• THE KINGDOM IS ABOUT SONSHIP

• THE KINGDOM IS FOR OVERCOMERS

Rev 21:7 He that overcometh shall inherit all things; and I will be his God, and he shall be my son.

In Revelation one, the Son of man is walking between the candlesticks holding seven stars in his hand. The voice commanded John to write to the seven churches, revealing to them how to become overcomers. To every church, He writes that the one that can hear what the Spirit says will be an overcomer. To every overcomer, their reward is spelled out; THE KINGDOM.

In chapter four, a Door was opened in heaven, and now we find the candlesticks lit up with flames. THE CHURCH IS BORN, the people who will possess the kingdom.

The Kingdom is a spiritual realm of authority and ruler ship, brought down to earth. It now operates on earth. It manifests itself only to those who are led by the Spirit and that is what whole of creation is waiting for, the manifestation of the sons of God right here on earth.

God's plan has always been to dwell in and with man. This plan was steadily revealed through the ages and opened once and for all, when the old was finally removed, that is what revelation is about.

> **Heb 9:8** the Holy Spirit indicating this, that the way into the Holiest of All was not yet made manifest while the first tabernacle was still standing.

> **Rev 15:8** The temple was filled with smoke from the glory of God and from His power, and no one was able to enter the temple till the seven plagues of the seven angels were completed.

The removal of the old started in Babylon and it gradually worked through all four empires and the final removal happened in one day when Rome burned down the temple.

> **Rev 16:1** And I heard a great voice out of the temple saying to the seven angels, Go your ways, and pour out the vials of the wrath of God upon the earth.

On the Cross Jesus cried, "It is finished." The temple in heaven was opened, but it was only after the total removal of the old system of the law, that it was thrown open. 70 AD, marks this point in time, when the the old system of sacrifices was finally removed.

Rev 21:6 And he said unto me, It is done. I am Alpha and Omega, the beginning and the end. I will give unto him that is athirst of the fountain of the water of life freely.

The Spirit now cries, "It is done." Nothing can hinder anyone from entering now, except Deception.

Mixing up the prophesies and the times in the Bible, is a serious mistake that will cause you to miss what God has for your day and age. A whole generation died in the desert, but God's Word came true, the same way, only believers will possess the Kingdom here. John the last apostle was the first to step into the Kingdom.

Rev 1:9 I John, who also am your brother, and companion in tribulation, and in the kingdom and patience of Jesus Christ,

Rev 21:3 And I heard a great voice out of heaven saying, Behold, the tabernacle of God [is] with men, and he will dwell with them, and they shall be his people, and God himself shall be with them, [and be] their God.

• THE OPERATION OF THE KINGDOM

There are two Kingdoms and they are two Spiritual realms: the Kingdom of darkness and the Kingdom of light. It is very easy to determine if you are operating in the right Kingdom.

The Kingdom of God;

- is not eating and drinking.
- is righteousness, peace, and joy in the Holy Ghost.

You have to Test yourself to see whether or not you are in Christ, for it is that place in the Spirit.

> **2 Cor 13:5** Examine yourselves as to whether you are in the faith. Test yourselves. Do you not know yourselves, that Jesus Christ is in you?-unless indeed you are disqualified.

You have to test yourself or you will be tested and this is the part no-one really wants, but it is for your own good. We are to be overcomers, not fire fighters.

> **1 Cor 3:13** each one's work will become clear; for the Day will declare it, because it will be revealed by fire; and the fire will test each one's work, of what sort it is.
> :14 If anyone's work which he has built on it endures, he will receive a reward.
> :15 If anyone's work is burned, he will suffer loss; but he himself will be saved, yet so as through fire.

THERE ARE MANY PEOPLE WHO SEE THE KINGDOM, BUT THEY NEVER ENTER.

Entering the Kingdom is through water and spirit, which is fire. The earth was cursed for man's sake and he had to till the ground to bring forth food. We need water and energy for seed to germinate, so man struggled against these elements. The kingdom is a place where there is no more curses and water and fire does not bring destruction.

Isa 43:2 When thou passest through the waters, I [will b with thee; and through the rivers, they shall not overflow thee: when thou walkest through the fire, thou shalt not be burned; neither shall the flame kindle upon thee.

Reading chapter twenty-one and twenty-two in Revelation, one can easily place this in the future, one day, somewhere beyond the blue; when we all get to heaven.

The blessing comes when you understand that this is the place that God has prepared for you, right here, right now and you may enter anytime. No matter what happens, it is a place of no more tears and death. Death is no more the end and we do not mourn as those who have no hope. Nothing can separate you from God, not life or death. The sting of death is removed.

The only tense you can use here is the Perfect Present tense. Past and future belongs to the natural mind. However, in the Spirit, past and future becomes one. This is the only place where you can forget what is behind, and nothing that happened or went wrong, can stop you from this wonderful communion with your Creator and lover of your Soul.

It seems too good to be true, especially looking at our situations in this fallen creation, however; we are supposed to be looking at Christ. It is a place where you actually believe, what you believe. That is why your mind has to transformed, and your eyes focused on Christ. As soon as you have stepped from darkness to light, you have stepped from death to life and it is a life that will never end. Your eternal life starts at your rebirth. Your spirit is already made perfect, which is the earnest or guarantee on your inside, pressing and urging you onward unto the redemption of the body.

> **Eph 1:14** That [Spirit] is the guarantee of our inheritance [the first fruits, the pledge and foretaste, the down payment on our heritage], in anticipation of its full redemption and our acquiring [complete] possession of it-to the praise of His glory.

• THE SPIRIT OF THE BOOK

The book of Revelation takes us into this finished work of the Christ and reveals a life of victory within this fallen creation. It is a New way of life where the old is gone; it reveals a new heaven and a New earth, a place where God dwells with man and sin has no effect anymore. It is a place where the pain is removed and curses have no effect. You can only experience it in this life, by and through the Spirit.

> **Rev 21:5** Then He who sat on the throne said, "Behold, I make all things new." And He said to me, "Write, for these words are true and faithful."
> **Rev 21:6** And He said to me, "It is done! I am the Alpha and the Omega, the Beginning and the End. I will give of the fountain of the water of life freely to him who thirsts.-
> **Rev 21:7** He who overcomes shall inherit all things, and I will be his God and he shall be My son.

Jesus told His disciples, in the sermon on the mount, that they were a "City set on a Hill", knowing that they were going to betray Him, steal from Him and even deny Him. He looked past all the human characteristics and gave them His plan for them; a "City set on a Hill".

In Revelation twenty-one, John describes this city in detail and calls it the "Bride of the Lamb", the "New Jerusalem", with twelve gates, which are the old testament tribes, and twelve foundation stones, which are the new testament apostles of the lamb.

Revelation twenty-two takes us right back to the river of God that flows in the middle of the highway of holiness surrounded by trees with leaves that bring healing to the nations.

> **Psa 1:3** (Message) You're a tree replanted in Eden, bearing fresh fruit every month, never dropping a leaf, always in blossom.

Revelation is not about the anti-Christ, it reveals the kingdom; the final outcome of God's working through the ages. It is a place of freedom, openness, and provision, where God himself, is the source of this light and life. The Spirit urges the church to be overcomers and this place is promised to all who overcomes, but it can only be encountered in the Spirit.

> **Rev 22:4** And they shall see his face; and his name [shall be] in their foreheads. (The way they think)

Moses spoke to God face to face and requested to see God's glory. While he was face to face with God, he was informed that he could not see God's face. This seems strange, till you look at the meaning of "face". The word for face is the word, 'Pawneem", the front side or forward side.

Moses only saw God's backside, he could not see the full plan of God, for he was not filled with the spirit. Flesh and blood cannot see the Kingdom, nor enter the Kingdom.

> **2 Co 3:16** Nevertheless when it shall turn to the Lord, the vail shall be taken away.
> :17 Now the Lord is that Spirit: and where the Spirit of the Lord is, there is liberty.
> :18 But we all, with open face beholding as in a glass the glory of the Lord, are changed into the same image from glory to glory, even as by the Spirit of the Lord.

JESUS CHRIST IS THE FACE OF GOD.

> **Rev 22:5** And there shall be no night there; and they need no candle, neither light of the sun; for the Lord God giveth them light: and they shall reign for ever and ever.
> **Rev 22:6** And he said unto me, These sayings [are] faithful and true: and the Lord God of the holy prophets sent his angel to shew unto his servants the things which must shortly be done.

The same Spirit that once hovered over the water now agrees with our spirit and will ultimately quicken out bodies and we will forever be in that state of perfection. Revelation is the consummation of what was started in the garden.

Rev 22:14

Blessed are they that do his commandments,

that they may have right to the tree of life,
and may enter in through the gates into the city.

Rev 22:17
And the Spirit and the bride say, Come.
And let him that heareth say, Come.
And let him that is athirst come.
And whosoever will, let him take the water of life freely.

Rev 22:20
He which testifieth these things saith,
Surely I come quickly. Amen.
Even so, come, Lord Jesus.

Rev 22:21
The grace of our Lord Jesus Christ be with you all. Amen.